Social Media Marketing and Facebook Marketing

Michael Branding

Published by Online Creative Services, 2021.

While every precaution has been taken in the preparation of this book, the publisher assumes no responsibility for errors or omissions, or for damages resulting from the use of the information contained herein.

SOCIAL MEDIA MARKETING AND FACEBOOK MARKETING

First edition. January 19, 2021.

ISBN: 978-1393144335

Written by Michael Branding.

Social Media Marketing and Facebook Marketing

Turn Your Business or Personal Brand Online Presence into a Money Making Machine with Facebook Advertising - An Easy Step by Step Facebook Ads Guide

By

Michael Branding

Chapter 1 - Basic Concepts

Social media marketing is a powerful way for businesses, professionals and organizations of all sizes to find and connect with returning or potential customers or users. Social marketers thus create company Facebook pages and accounts on Twitter, Instagram, Pinterest and other major social networks to reach this goal.

However, not all of these professionals really have clear goals and well defined strategies, nor an in-depth knowledge of how social media interact with consumers and how they can use this interaction to increase brand awareness, boost sales and profits, and create brand loyalty. This is why we strongly recommend that you understand how social media marketing actually works and deeply study the content of this book, as it has everything you need to know to turn your online presence into a money making machine.

Knowing the ABC of social media marketing, having understood exactly what social media marketing is, how it works, how much it requires in terms of time, human resources and budget, is the fundamental premise for those who want to do social marketing in a professional and effective way. This is why it is important to get started by having a clear and exhaustive definition of social media marketing. Knowing the field you are moving on is the best way to avoid big mistakes, especially at the beginning stages. Whether you want to build your personal brand or are looking for resources to boost your company presence online, you cannot skip this first important step.

So, let's get started.

Social media marketing or SMM (also known as social network marketing, social marketing, and, by extension, also facebook marketing, linkedin marketing, etc...) is a branch of online marketing applied to social networks. This discipline exploits the ability of social media and web-social applications (apps) to generate interaction (engagement) and social sharing, in order to increase the visibility and notoriety of a brand, a product or service, a freelancer or a public figure. It includes activities such as the promotion and sale of particular goods and services, the generation of new business contacts (which are called "leads") and the increase in traffic to a brand's official website or social pages.

For promotional purposes it is good to integrate a social media marketing strategy with other forms of online marketing, such as: Search Engine Marketing (SEM), Social Media Optimization (SMO), Social Media Advertising (SMA) or Social ads, and Public digital relations or Digital Pr.

Social media marketing, together with social customer service, social selling and other branches of digital marketing, is considered a component of Social Business, since it also includes pay-per-click marketing activities.

Companies and organizations create, or connect to, "networks of individuals" (communities) that share interests and values expressed by the company on social networks. Then, they use these online communities to offer their users relevant content in various formats (mainly text, images and videos) in order to stimulate discussions around the brand.

This is the concrete expression of a very important marketing principle: when people speak about a company, that company can take advantage of the attention, no matter what people say about the company.

In fact, if managed correctly, user and customer interaction with these contents can produce loyalty and social media advocacy. Users and customers, with their "likes", "comments" and "shares" activate word of mouth online by individually involving their network (friends, fans and followers) in the discussion. If you have a company, you know how powerful word of mouth is. Now imagine how big of an impact it can have on your business, when you take it online, where there is virtually no limit on the amount of people one single individual can enter in contact with.

This greatly increases the possibility that a percentage of them ends up becoming a fan or follower of the company or the brand.

An important distinction: Social marketing or social media marketing?

Sometimes on blogs, podcasts and other online content, social marketing is mistakenly used as a synonym for social media marketing. In reality, social marketing is a popular discipline that became famous in the early 1970s thanks to Philip Kotler and Gerald Zaltman. When we are talking about social marketing, the "product" to be promoted is not a good or a service but is "human behavior". The goal of a social advertising campaign is in fact, for example, to encourage people to protect the environment or to fight against racism.

It is just a simple distinction, but it is important to keep this in mind as in this book we are always referring to social media marketing, not social marketing.

Chapter 2 - Advantages and Disadvantages of Social Media Marketing

Now that we have discussed and understood the definition of social media marketing, let's try to understand what benefits it can bring to a company or a personal brand. Here is a list of the main reasons why social media marketing is one of the greatest tools available to anyone that wants to do business online.

- Improvement of customer satisfaction. It has been proven that clients that can get in contact with the brand behind their favourite product are more likely to report a positive shopping experience and become returning customers.

- Increase in customer loyalty (brand loyalty). As mentioned above, people that can see a powerful online presence tend to deem that brand as "solid" and "reliable", which inevitably translates to more money for the company.

- Customer service improvement. Having a good social media presence can help a brand to give a better customer service to its clients by answering their questions directly on the different platforms. Furthermore, this behaviour improves the reliability of the company and helps people that are on the fence to become paying customers.

- Increase in sales leads and sales. As we will see in the coming chapters, social media marketing can be used to actively increase the number of leads and sales, thanks to online advertising tools.

- Increase in web traffic to the company site or personal blog. This is easy to understand. When you attract the attention of someone, you can redirect that attention wherever you want. Your or your company website is a good choice in most cases.

● Better positioning of your siteì on search engines. This is closely connected with the previous point. When you direct the attention you attract on social media to a website, that website becomes more interesting for Google and other search engines. Therefore, it is not a surprise that social media marketing is also a great way to increase the organic reach of the brand website.

● Increase in brand awareness. This really needs no comment. Brand awareness, as we will see in the coming chapters, is extremely important in this day and age.

● Connection and development of interactive relationships with your target audience. Being able to engage with your target audience is truly an incredible gift, as it allows you to better understand your customers' needs and satisfy them with your amazing product or service.

● Development of a reputation as an expert or leader in the relevant sector (brand authority). By improving your social presence, you improve the view that the general public has of your brand. Think about Apple or Tesla: they have an amazing social presence and they are considered by everyone the leader in their sector.

But is it all sunshines and rainbows?

Well, that could not be farther from the truth. In fact, social media marketing also presents some difficulties to the newcomers, but they are all manageable with the right skills. Before diving deeper, we would like to point out some point of resistance that you or your brand may face when getting started.

● Lack of resources. Social networks are varied and different, consequently the various forms of content (text, video, podcast, webinar, etc.) that have to be published and shared must be adapted to the specificities of each one of them. Likewise, a social media marketing campaign cannot be launched and left alone. It requires time and human resources dedicated to it, in order to be profitable in the long run.

This is the reason why, at a certain point, especially for many small companies and personal brands, social media marketing becomes too expensive. By continuing reading this book you will understand how you can reduce the costs, while still building an impactful online presence.

• Negative feedback from your customers. When we discussed the advantages of social media marketing, we stated that word of mouth is an amazing tool to boost sales. Well, that is true if people are talking positively about you. The opposite effect comes when people start giving bad feedback. This can escalate quickly and can lead to a substantial loss of users or clients.

You can avoid this in many ways, but the best one is to have a truly amazing product.

Chapter 3 - The Importance of Social Media Marketing

So, we have now come to the most important question of them all. Why should a company or personal brand invest in social media marketing? Let's discuss some points together.

- Low costs. Creating profiles on social networks is free as well as creating and managing social media campaigns with your own social media management team.

- High ROI (return on investment) from advertising costs. The ROI generated by social media advertising is the highest among the various forms of paid advertising. Furthermore, social ads are a type of advertising that allows for high target profiling and personalization. This means that the ads will only be shown to users who are really interested in products or services promoted by the advertiser. This is crucial, as it allows you to cut out everyone that is not in target with what you are offering.

- High conversion rate (CR). More than 51% of social media marketers say that developing meaningful relationships with customers has a positive impact on sales results. This inevitably increases the conversion rate of advertising.

- Improvement of customer insights. Unlike content shared through private channels such as e-mails, instant messaging tools and apps, which are therefore difficult to measure, various social media marketing tools allow precise monitoring of activities on various social networks. From the analysis of the numerous data collected (insight) using tools such as Google Analytics, it is possible to obtain important information on the "sentiment" towards the brand, as well as on the demographic composition, interests, behaviors and needs of customers.

The importance of Social Media Marketing for businesses and personal brands
Why is social media marketing important? Social networks have become a virtual meeting place for people, where:

- they exchange ideas on the most disparate topics.

- they read reviews on products and services they want to buy.

- they look for information on places they want to go, such as restaurants or hotels.

Once, when these social platforms did not exist, this exchange of news took place in clubs or in other social gathering spaces. Today, however, people spend much more time on Instagram, Facebook, YouTube or LinkedIn and that is where they often "meet" and talk to each other. What does this mean? This means that companies and professionals should increasingly work on the ability to intercept and engage users in discussions on online social networks, because in these online environments it is possible to make them become their customers. People's opinions are increasingly influenced by conversations on the internet and this is a fact to take into account if you are selling a product on the web, if you are marketing online, or even if you just want to become important and relevant as an influencer.

Why does this trend affect us? If you are a businessman, or an online marketer, to reach your audience - which is your potential customer base - you must become good at getting noticed where they can find you. And by now you should have understood that that place is online. You must be present and be able to influence the opinions of those who have to make purchasing decisions and you have to do that online, because it is there that purchasing decisions are made more and more frequently.

Chapter 4 - Social Media Marketing as a Career

If you are not an entrepreneur that wants to take their company online, but you are just starting to look at social media marketing as a career opportunity, just know that being proficient on social media is also important for those looking for new professional opportunities. This will help you to:

● find a job in a fresh and up to date company;

● be desired by businesses all around the world. In fact, the internet has destroyed physical boundaries and companies look for talents from all around the world, thanks to the possibility given by smart working;

● have career opportunities and increasing earnings. You have to know that social media managers are paid very well, especially if they can provide concrete results to the company they are working for.

To be interesting and attractive to companies, it will also be appropriate to become good at handling the different software, tools and platforms through which you can reach users interested in a product or service on social networks.

Who is the social media marketer?

The Social media marketer (or social media manager) is a digital marketing professional who manages and supervises the social media, digital media and social network channels within a company and acts as a connection between a community of users and the company itself.

He is also responsible for designing the content strategy, managing social media marketing campaigns on Facebook, Twitter and other social networks with the help of the social media team; the creation of an editorial plan with a view to seo; the promotion of products, services and events, and sharing the contents of the company website or blog. In small and medium-sized businesses, the role of the social media marketer is delegated to figures usually subordinate to him such as:

- Web Content Editor
- Community Manager
- Social Media Specialist
- Digital Marketing Manager
- Digital PR Manager
- Social media strategist
- Facebook Ads Specialist
- Social Customer Care Specialist

Chapter 5 - Social Media Marketing in 7 Steps

There are various ways in which a company or organization can do social media marketing. However, all social media marketing activities carried out to be effective cannot be separated from the implementation of an effective social media marketing strategy. But how to define and set up a successful social media marketing strategy?

As in any digital marketing strategy, this is developed through the definition of a social media marketing plan which consists of some precise phases. Let's take a closer look at each one of them.

Please, note that this chapter serves a general structure for the key concept that will be discussed later on in the book.

Step 1 - Conducting a social media marketing audit

In this first step, the audit activity is aimed at evaluating the digital assets (blog, site, app, etc.) available, also in relation to the competition, in order to detect on each social channel what works and what does not work.

In order to simplify this process, here is a list of a few questions that you should aim to answer in this first step. Be as precise as possible, as it will dictate the fundamental aspects of your social media marketing strategy.

- On which social platforms is the brand currently active?

- Which social networks carry the most value?

- What kind of content do competitors post?

- What tone of voice did they choose?

- How much traffic to the website does each social channel bring?

- What types of content do we post on the different channels? How frequently?

- Are we getting results from investing in social media advertising?

Step 2 - Definition of your social media marketing goals

Having analyzed the digital assets, audience and competition, the next step in establishing an effective social media strategy concerns the definition of goals and results that you hope to achieve (number of leads, customer loyalty, increased sales, brand awareness, etc.)

These goals need to be aligned with the overall communication and marketing strategy so that social media enables the achievement of business goals. In setting goals, to ensure that these will be achieved, it is good to follow the SMART method (specific, measurable, feasible, realistic, as a function of time) used for the first time by Drucker in 1954, in the book "The practice of Management".

Step 3 - Identification of your target audience

You need to be clear who your target audience is so that the message you want to convey on social media is effective. Developing typical customer profiles (buyer personas) is essential for the development of a social media marketing strategy. The collection and analysis of data on the web or from conducting online surveys allow the marketer to paint a well rounded profile of the typical customer. Once the audience has been defined, through surveying activities, they can understand on which social platforms the customer (real or potential) is present.

How do you define your target audience?

We have a dedicated chapter in this book, but let's get a simple idea in order to better understand phase 4.

The surveying activity can be carried out with the help of some social media monitoring tools for marketing automation or manually. Let's briefly see with this last method how to do surveying on Facebook, Twitter and LinkedIn:

1. Write down a list of keywords that are meaningful to you that indicate your product, service, brand or need that you can satisfy.
2. Enter the chosen keyword in the search field of the social network and wait for the results. In the search box you can filter them by "main results", "people", "pages", "places", "groups", "applications" and "events".
3. Enter the following data relating to the comments obtained (date, author, influence, sentiment) in an excel file and store it. This will give you an overview of what is being said online about the chosen brand or topic.

Step 4 - Creating a social media content strategy

Contents are very important in order to create engagement and to achieve your social media marketing goals. With this in mind, it is essential to follow a strategic approach focused on the creation and distribution of relevant and valuable content (Content Marketing), aimed at a clearly defined audience. This is why it is important to do step 3 before starting to produce content without a target audience in mind.

For the communication strategy on the various social media to be effective, however, it will be good to plan the management of these contents. This process is called content strategy and it requires an editorial plan.

For the planning of the editorial plan it can be useful to draw up a matrix of the contents or to use the 80/20 rule of Pareto. In the latter case, 80% of the posts must be used to inform, train or entertain their audience, while the remaining 20% to promote the brand. As for the frequency of publication, given that quality beats quantity, for a small company 2 or 3 weekly contents are generally sufficient. Here are some of the most popular types of content:

- Infographics
- Articles
- Images
- Videos
- Ebooks
- Interviews
- Institutional or corporate news announcements
- Live and virtual events
- Assistance (customer care)

Step 5: Pay attention to Influencers

Research carried out on Twitter shows that 49% of consumers rely on the advice of Influencers in making purchasing decisions. Finding those who have a large social following for recommendations on the products or services you sell is therefore very important for the success of your social media marketing strategy. One way for a company to gain visibility with social influencers is to use the sharing system suggested by Joe Pulizzi and the Content Marketing Institute, known as Social Media 4-1-1. For every 6 content shared via social media, 4 must be relevant content for your target audience but written by influencers; 1 must be original content created by us; 1 content must be about the sale of your product or service (a coupon for example). You can see how Joe Pulizzi agrees with the Pareto Principle as well.

To engage influencers, I invite you to also take into account any affiliate program to propose to those who are part of your niche. Affiliate marketing, in fact, provides for the payment of a commission to an intermediary, in this case the influencer, for each sale or lead that it manages to generate among its audience. This translates into a win-win situation. The influencer is happy because he can get a portion of the revenues generated and the company is happy because it can get sales without spending money.

Step 6 - Choosing the social media marketing platform

A social media marketing strategy must also be planned taking into account the market in which the company operates (B2B or B2C), the purchasing decision-making phase (social consumer decision journey) in which the customer may possibly be found (research, consideration, decision). Knowing the differences between the platforms and identifying the best ones to support the company's marketing objectives is fundamental. So let's take a brief look at the most famous social networks, not focusing on what these social media are, but in relation to the marketing activities that can be implemented with them.

Facebook

With almost 2.1 billion users and a growth of 15% (year-on-year figure), it is one of the largest social networks in the world. With this social platform it is possible to precisely identify your target audience, create engagement starting from Facebook Groups, easily implement real alternative advertising campaigns to Adwords. The possibility of integrating content in various formats into Facebook is endless and recently it is also possible by clicking on a special button to integrate Instagram content. Users of MailChimp, an email marketing software, can then natively create Facebook ads from their account.

Facebook has many arrows in its bow (Facebook media, Facebook business manager, Facebook live, Facebook connect, Facebook Stories, Facebook news feed ads, Facebook video ads). Let's briefly see the characteristics of some of them:

- Facebook Ads. Advertising on Facebook allows you to reach a conversion rate of 30% higher than other social platforms and allows a decrease in costs per conversion of 50%

- Facebook Places. Is the Facebook geo-location service that allows the user to add information about the place where he is, and based on this, find places, information of interest divided by category (restaurants, shops, entertainment, etc.) and friends who are nearby.

The presence of "tiles" or boxes that refer to company fan pages make it a valuable tool for social media marketing activities.

● Facebook media. It is a tool used to teach users who have created fan pages on Facebook to manage them effectively. To access Facebook media just connect to media.fb.com.

● Facebook bluetooth beacons. The social network provides devices applicable to a physical area of your business (beacons) that allow you to send marketing communications (promotional offers, etc.) via smartphone to potential customers who pass in your vicinity. To request beacons, you must register on their waiting list.

● Facebook business manager. Is a free and easy to use tool for advertising and marketing on Facebook. From its dashboard it is possible to monitor the performance of anything connected to your business on Facebook.

Another particularity offered by Facebook is the possibility given to marketers to create effective advertising campaigns aimed at a relatively small audience through Dark Marketing activities. Through a Chrome app (Power Editor) it is possible to create "dark posts" on Facebook. In short, Facebook gives advertisers the ability to create sponsored posts that do not appear on the user's timeline but are accessible to anyone with a direct link or by clicking from an ad.

Instagram

Instagram is a photo sharing application for iPhone, Android and Windows platforms. At the heart of Instagram social media marketing are Instagram stories. They are a way to share photos and videos with your followers that will no longer be visible after 24 hours. Instagram lends itself a lot to social web marketing: people post images and videos, tag friends, insert hashtags and click on content shared by others, making Instagram the social network with the highest engagement rate.

On Instagram it is also possible to post a new type of post called "shoppable post" which includes a special tag that connects the objects in the photo directly to the corresponding e-commerce. Instagram is now testing a new "nametags" feature similar to Snapchat's Snapcodes or Messenger code that makes it easier to acquire Instagram followers. Its "visual" features make this social network suitable for b2b social media marketing, such as travel business, e-commerce and social events.

LinkedIn

LinkedIn is one of the best professional social platforms to connect with your network of collaborators (Linkedin groups) and potential future employers. The social network allows users to import contacts and integrates services such as SlideShare and Pulse. Today LinkedIn is the most popular social network for professionals in the world and is considered the most effective B2B social media marketing and lead generation platform. Like other social platforms, also on Linkedin it is possible to manage advertisements (Linkedin ads). The platform also offers businesses and publishers the ability to natively run video ad campaigns and include videos within their company pages. Through the implemented Linkedin Tracking pixel, it is then possible to measure the number of leads, sign-ups, visits to websites and other actions generated by video ads.

Snapchat

Snapchat is a mobile application that allows users to send photos and videos to friends. Snapchat Stories (collages of photos and videos shared for no more than 24 hours) are a great engagement tool. With the release of the new version of the app, it will soon be possible to share Snapchat stories also on Facebook and Twitter. Snapchat is testing new in-app e-commerce options through its Snap store located within the Discover platform, which could lead to partnerships with companies of all kinds in the future. If your products are aimed at a very young audience, marketing on Snapchat is definitely the right choice.

Pinterest

Pinterest is a popular photo sharing service that allows anyone to create collections and more. 93% of its users use it to plan purchases or to research product information. Marketing activities are possible thanks to Pinterest ads and buyable pins. Pinterest is continuing to grow among small and medium enterprises. The adhesions to its Pinterest Propel program in fact recorded a + 50% this year. With 81% of its 150 million monthly active users being women, topics such as interior design, decoration, cooking and clothing work very well.

Reddit

Reddit is the social network where the community decides what will be more relevant and what to give more visibility to. Reddit has a subreddit (think of it as a digital board) for almost every category. The growth of this social network in the world is due to 2 factors: the AMAs format (ask me everything) and the peculiarities of the voting system. Marketing activities are possible thanks to Reddit ads, however, it is necessary to pay close attention to the large number of comments received and therefore it requires constant attention.

Telegram

Telegram is a messaging application that allows you to chat with contacts, organizing public and private groups, with a series of functions dedicated to visual content. You can add images, emojis, documents, files and links to messages. Companies can use Telegram to notify their clients of new offers and promotions or to directly chat with them if we are talking about a small and close community.

Tumblr

Tumblr is a microblogging platform with social networking features. Much used by fashion brands, bloggers and designers for the publication of very accurate content. People spend more time on this platform than on Facebook, which makes Tumblr a good place to post and advertise.

Twitter

Twitter is another fantastic social media platform that allows users to quickly send 280-character posts through Tweets. These are characterized by the presence in the text of an hashtag (a keyword preceded by the hash symbol #). Twitter marketing is often used by companies to maintain contact with their customers, to promote their brands, products or services, and to obtain information from consumers.

Whatsapp

Whatsapp is one of the most used instant messaging applications in the world given the ease of use and quality of service. In 2017 WhatsApp crossed the milestone of 1 billion users per day, thus equaling Facebook. The app offers the possibility of interacting with your contacts within conversations and today you can publish, as status updates, temporary Snapchat-style photos and videos. With the release this year of WhatsApp Business, and the coming integration of the possibility of making payment, the brand officially accesses one-to-one marketing.

Disqus

Disqus was born as a commentary hosting service for websites and blogs. This platform now represents a real social network where users can give life to debates or participate in existing ones. To manage comments, just access the platform with the same account used for social media, using the "share" button you can then bring the discussion to your favorite social network.

YouTube

Youtube is a network where users post video blogs, video ads and videos of various genres. For marketers, videos are the ideal medium to share medium to long-form content and Youtube is the go to hosting place for video content.

Step 7 - Measurement and testing

It is necessary to constantly analyze the social media marketing strategies implemented to understand which has been effective and which has not. As part of a social media marketing strategy, it is necessary to decide which metrics or KPIs to use to verify whether the set goals have been achieved. Some metrics to consider to measure the success of a social media marketing strategy are the following:

- Cost per click (CPA)
- Conversion Rate
- Number of followers
- Brand mention
- Total shares
- Impressions
- Comments and engagement

Chapter 6 - Social Media Marketing Trends for 2021

Social media are dynamic by their nature and, for this reason, they are characterized by trends and communication methods that can vary over time (ever heard about social media trends). Knowing these trends can be crucial in choosing the most direct and effective social media marketing strategies. Below is a brief description of the social media marketing strategies that, as it seems, will most characterize 2021.

1. Use Tik Tok for your Social Media Marketing strategy. This social network is growing rapidly and is a must for those who want to reach users under 30, which currently represents 66% of the channel's users.

2. Social media wellness becomes essential to create engagement among users. People are gaining greater awareness of the use of social networks and the impact they have on mental health. This is why even the platforms themselves are committed to making the user experience pleasant and not very harmful. If you notice changes in the level of engagement, you should not be scared, but observe your competitors and if they suffer the same reduction you can feel comfortable. People are increasingly trying to reduce their time on social media and leverage the time they spend constructively.

3. Fake news will be limited. This is certainly excellent news and a very positive trend. The fact that fake news is on the decline does not mean that it still does not remain a problem. For those involved in social media marketing this means that the user will weigh heavily what you declare about your company and your products. So, please, maximum transparency!

4. Tightened security. Another growing trend strongly correlated to social media marketing is user security. The recent scandal involving Facebook and Cambridge Analytica is likely to further enhance this trend. The privacy protection measures for users of Social networks will have to be increasingly suitable to fight hacking, identity theft, phishing and various other security threats.

5. A more effective strategy with augmented reality and virtual reality. Technology is taking great steps towards AR and VR and you must be able to adapt to this change. Augmented reality and virtual reality will improve not only the effectiveness of your strategy, but also the experience of your users.

6. The use of artificial intelligence will increase. The use of artificial intelligence (chatbots and virtual assistants) will increasingly allow marketers to interact with consumers in real time and in a personalized way. Facebook is preparing to relaunch a virtual assistant that will be able to offer suggestions to users and answer all their requests through the Facebook Messenger chat. According to Gartner, a world-leading multinational company in strategy consulting, research and analysis in the field of Information Technology (IT), 20% of business content could be generated this year by machines similar to artificial intelligence. Think about it, of every ten articles you read online, two of them are probably written by a robot.

7. Designing the social media marketing strategy to involve Generation Z. The generation of the future is becoming more and more involved with technology and this requires innovation and creativity from marketers. 2021 will be the year of the challenge to find new ways to entertain and involve the youngest, studying them carefully and understanding their needs.

8. Influencer Marketing. Social media influencers are able to generate a return on investment 11 times greater than any other digital marketing strategy. It is no coincidence that 94% of social media marketers claim to have achieved excellent results thanks to their collaboration and consider them an integral part of their social media marketing strategy.

In recent years, this tactic has been used in many sectors (social media marketing for tourism is an example above all), with results such as to become the main digital channel for many companies. The success and evolution of this tactic has also favored the creation of numerous new professional figures. Among the most sought after we find the social media marketer.

Chapter 7 - SMART Method for Goal Setting

Here is a quick overview of the SMART method.

Specific, measurable, attainable, realistic and time effective: this is how goals should be formulated, so that they are effective for the purposes of our planning and organization work. Use the SMART method for formulating goals. In this way, all the criteria that a well-formulated goal must possess will be respected.

The aim is to create an exceptional planning and organization process. Knowing what we want to achieve with our social media marketing strategy is important, but how do we state that clearly so that we can increase the odds of actually achieving our goals?

This is where the SMART method comes into place. As mentioned before, SMART is an acronym and indicates the criteria for the formulation of a goal, which must therefore be specific, measurable, attainable, realistic and have a specific time period.

Specific goals

We often make the first mistake by not reflecting deeply on what we want to achieve with our social media marketing strategy and we favor an inadequately specific formulation of our goals.

Examples of non-specific objectives:

"We want to make more money."

"We want more followers."

What do these statements mean? When is it "in the future"? And how much would you like to increase the number of followers? What does it mean to make more money? Does it refer to sales or profit? Neither objective specifies what the final perspective is. Take this into account when formulating your goal.

The same goals formulated specifically:

"In the next month, we want to increase our monthly revenue by 5% using social media marketing"

"In the next month, we will get at least 1000 more followers on our Instagram page."

Measurable goals

In order to verify the achievement of the goal or to get motivated to work towards it, the goal must be measurable.

Examples of non-measurable goals:

"We want to post beautiful images on our social media pages."

"We want to have good comments on our posts."

What does beautiful images mean? When do you deem a comment as good? Do not leave room for interpretation. Formulate the goal in such a way that it can be verified whether it has been achieved or not.

Examples of measurable goals:

"We want to post images on social media pages that get at least 1000 likes."

"We want to receive one positive feedback every two customers."

Attainable goals

In order not to give up on your goals, it is necessary that you recognize them as such and accept it. In other words: the goal must be attractive to your or your company eyes.

Examples of unattainable goals:

"During the week we will post 100 times per day."

"In the future, all customer inquiries will be dealt with immediately."

Be honest with yourself. Can you accept these goals? Will they be attractive enough to your eyes even over a period of months? Set goals in such a way that for you personally and for all employees they are actually achievable and remain attractive over time.

Examples of attainable goals:

"We dedicate myself to our social channels consistently, posting at least 5 times per day to create brand awareness."

"All customer inquiries will be processed within 48 hours."

Realistic goals

In the throes of ambition, we have the feeling of being able to achieve anything. But even then, be honest with yourself. Are you able and are you willing to achieve these goals and keep chipping at them?

Examples of unrealistic goals:

"At the end of the day we always respond to all the comments we received that day."

"From now on we will always refund our customers."

Don't be fooled by your ambition when formulating goals. Stay realistic to avoid bankruptcy in the short term.

Examples of realistic goals:

"We organize our comment according to priorities (1 = urgent / 2 = to be fulfilled within 2 days / 3 = to be fulfilled by the end of the week) and we make sure that at the end of the day we have carried out the tasks of priority 1."

"We will refund customers that actually are suitable for the refund, based on the contract they signed when they made the purchase."

Time effective goals

Don't leave the deadline of your goal to chance.

Examples of non time effective goals:

"We will post on our social channels."

"We will answer those comments."

You now have unlimited time to do those two things. Sooner or later these goals will be reached. However, you prefer to define in the goal itself the deadline by which you want to reach it or put it into practice:

Examples of time effective goals:

"We will post on our social channels by 9am every day."

"We will answer those comments before lunch."

Think about the SMART method the next time you formulate goals for your social media marketing strategy and write them down. In this way it will be easier for you not to lose sight of them and to achieve them faster.

Chapter 8 - Pareto Principle and the Yerkes and Dodson Curve

The Pareto principle is also called the "80/20 law" or the "Pareto effect". Regardless of how you decide to call it, the principle is named after its discoverer Vilfredo Pareto (1848-1923). At the beginning of the 20th century, Pareto, an engineer, sociologist and economist, conducted research concerning the subdivision of popular heritage in Italy. Pareto's research showed that one fifth, or 20% of Italian citizens, had about 80% of the national wealth.

Pareto therefore deduced that the banks should have concentrated on that 20% of Italians to be more efficient and obtain greater profits, thus indirectly establishing that the banks only devote a fifth of their time to assisting the remaining 80% of the population.

The Pareto principle represented the inequality of the division and the lack of balance between the resources used and profit. However, this proportion was also true in other sectors.

- Commerce: 20% of products or customers invoice 80% of earnings.
- Storage: 20% of products take up 80% of the places on the shelves.
- Internet: 80% of data traffic is generated on 20% of websites.
- Road transport: 80% of all journeys take place on 20% of roads.
- Phone calls: 80% of calls are made to and from 20% of the saved contacts

The 80/20 law is best known for its application in time management. Because with a correct setting of your time it is possible to do 80% of the work in 20% of the time taken.

The goal of the rule discovered by Pareto is to achieve the greatest result with the least effort, since a lot of time is often invested in tasks with lower priority. With the right priorities and better time management, however, you can set up your work more efficiently and in a targeted manner. The Pareto principle is particularly suitable for those professional sectors with tight deadlines, allowing you to focus your efforts in the most efficient way possible and to complete the tasks within the established time frame. This 80/20 law is usually associated with other methods of time management, such as the Eisenhower principle.

There are some types of errors that are often encountered in the application of the principle in question. The first is that it is wrongly claimed that with 20% of the time invested, 80% more than normal is reached, thus bringing the yield to 100%. This is clearly a misinterpretation, where the figures are added together, thus leading to 100%, despite the fact that they are actually two different and separate aspects. Commitment and performance are not the same thing and therefore cannot be added together so easily. To generate 100% of the yield you need to commit 100% and that is especially true when it comes to social media marketing.

An interpretation of this type serves no other purpose than to give false hopes, which are far too optimistic. However, understanding the functioning of the basic principle is not enough to avoid misinterpreting its use. In fact, one might be led to think, always wrongly, that it is enough to reduce all tasks to only 20%. But here too, we must not get confused: many of the jobs that need to be done in social media marketing do not lead directly to the goal, however they are necessary to get there. Writing and replying to emails fall within the duties of this type, which in fact, although they may seem a negligible element and of little relevance to the success of a company, are nevertheless essential.

The Pareto principle serves precisely to optimize those tasks that remain necessary despite generating less or no profit, so as to take away as little time as possible. Any incorrect use of the Pareto principle can lead to the attribution of too low importance to a large part of the work to be carried out. The fact is that only those who dedicate themselves to their work in a conscious, concentrated and structured manner can obtain 80% of the results with 20% of the work done. Social media marketing falls perfectly under this principle.

The 80/20 law is very versatile. It can be used in one's private life, in study and at work for better time management. In our case, we use it to develop a much more effective and time saving social media marketing strategy. The important thing is to know which activity contributes most to achieving what you want, so as to be able to give the right priority to the various tasks. The Pareto principle helps to make the best choice in this regard.

From a purely theoretical point of view, the Pareto principle can be applied in any sector, not only in social media marketing. It has seen successful application in school and academic training, as well as in everyday life for normal people. Often the 80/20 law is associated with the working life, where it is more usual to have strict deadlines and well defined goals. But even in everyday private life there are many tasks that must be carried out in a short time and as efficiently as possible.

An example for everyday life

In order to understand the importance of Pareto Principle for social media marketing optimization, it can be useful to take a look at a common everyday life scenario.

If friends or family tell you that they will be visiting you shortly, there is little time left to clean up the house. Normally, to put everything in order and carry out all the household chores, it usually takes three hours, but in the case of such a visit, it often takes no more than an hour and a half. For this reason, following what is determined by the Pareto principle, it is initially advisable to focus on those that contribute to the well-being of the guests. Collecting objects and clothes around the apartment, putting dirty dishes in the dishwasher and cleaning the table is part of these chores.

The rooms most often used by guests are the living room, bathroom and dining room, and are therefore the ones on which you need to focus initially. Cleaning these rooms practically corresponds to the aforementioned 80% of "success", while one's bedroom, cellar and the like alter the mood of guests to a lesser extent.

In social media marketing this translates, for instance, into taking care of the most important customer requests first, prioritizing them over the less urgent ones.

Yerkes and Dodson curve

Similarly to the Pareto principle, Yerkes and Dodson law also has to do with the relationship between commitment and productivity. The curve in question takes its name from psychologists Robert Yerkes and John Dodson. From their research it emerged that productivity improves proportionally according to the growth of the commitment, at least until the maximum point is reached, or the point where the improvement in performance reaches its maximum, thus leading to a decrease in productivity.

The Yerkes and Dodson curve is represented by an inverted U. Despite continuing to invest time and energy, productivity inevitably begins to decline once the top is reached. The high pressure and the resulting stress cause a decrease in performance, leading to worse results. Like the Pareto Principle, the Yerkes and Dodson law also affirms, or rather confirms, that only a certain part of the commitment leads to most of the productivity. The remaining effort required to achieve 100% results leads to very little in terms of productivity.

Chapter 9 - Identify the Correct Buyer Persona

As for every concept we introduce in this book, let's start by giving a detailed definition of what a buyer persona is and what it is not.

Buyer personas are fictitious representations of typical customers of a company, created on the basis of data collected through surveys or interviews, taking into account not only their socio-demographic, psychographic and behavioral characteristics but also data, quotes and sayings that can be useful for creating ad hoc products and services.

These are archetypes or models that result from insights provided by consumers and users. Making use of buyer personas therefore means starting from the study of real customers to guide business and marketing strategies that will lead to the involvement, conversion and loyalty of new buyers. The insights collected may concern various types of data, such as personal information, expressions used, ways of speaking and quotes, taken during interviews, which allow us to illustrate in a more "human" way, thus going beyond the numbers and statistics relating to purchases and preferences, the "type" of person who visits a site, page or shop.

All the information collected and analyzed makes it possible to create archetypes from which brands can align their marketing strategy and brand positioning based, therefore, on the expectations of current customers and potential buyers.

The identification of buyer personas includes the collection and analysis of socio-demographic data, data relating to purchasing habits, payment methods, and much more. These are in fact useful information but not exhaustive if you intend to accurately identify the customer or the typical user of a business. As many expert explain, very often when we try to identify buyer target we mainly think about a demographic target. Maybe we think about the gender, the age group, the geographical area which our users come from. The reality of the facts is that what works in terms of communication is not so much knowing this information but what the behavioral and motivational data of the macro-groups and segments of users who arrive on our site are.

Knowing what their problems are and how they would like to solve them is useful, as it allows us to collect data relating to the value system of users or customers in order to create targeted content that meets their way of thinking and to conceive of reality.

The use of the term personas, intended as the creation of typical profiles of users who visit a website, is attributed to Alan Cooper, software designer and programmer who, thanks to his experience in the field, has developed and studied over the years the application of this methodology to the design sector for the creation of user-friendly software. The result of these researches was initially published in 1998 in "The Inmates Are Running the Asylum", a book that introduced the concept which then spread widely in various sectors.

The reason behind the construction of a buyer persona

These profiles are useful for guiding the decision-making process relating to multiple aspects of the business, such as the creation and definition of the characteristics of products, services and store, the definition of the structure and layout of a site, as well as marketing strategies. Furthermore, they help identify the correct brand positioning to be adopted to communicate our services and products in an appropriate manner to the various customer groups.

The traditional approach of identifying the target of a product, service or message is based on the collection of mainly quantitative data, obtained thanks to statistical analysis and socio-demographic information, but also related to purchasing behavior and preferences by channel communication.

However, this type of survey is not enough to identify the psychological nuances of the average customer or user of a site, as many marketing experts have explained during the years. In fact, as the expert explains, even if the definition of the target is essential to understand what to focus the company resources on and to identify the aspects of the business that need to be optimized, this only allows to clarify " what" to propose, but not "how" to offer it to customers. In fact, in planning a marketing strategy it is necessary to create content aimed at the different targets of the business, since a generalist and not very personalized communication cannot be in line with the way of communicating and reasoning of different customers and, therefore, it will be difficult to respond. to different doubts, worries and needs.

To better understand your target and create content that is truly relevant to potential customers, it is advisable to think like them and try to identify with the different buyer personas and their "thought structures" as David Meerman Scott explains in the aforementioned book. In the same book, the author explained that "the idea behind the concept of buyer personas is to understand your target so well that you practically start to think like him".

Design the perfect buyer persona for your company

The creation of these archetypes allows us to understand who the customers or users of a site are, but also the way they think, what they want to achieve and what are the objectives and reasons that guide their behavior, in addition to the methods and timing of purchase. To construct the identikit of the ideal customer or user, it is necessary to take into account different types of information relating to consumers and proceed with the collection of data through survey tools that allow you to listen to customers and then, in a subsequent phase, process the data that will allow to identify and construct the different buyer personas in an accurate and detailed way.

What data to collect

In the collection of data for the construction of the representations of the customer or the ideal user of a site, we range from the most personal information (such as socio-demographic, psychographic data, etc.) to those that instead relate more specifically to any response, approach or preference of the typical customer towards a product, a site or a company.

Socio-demographic data

Socio-demographic data allow you to "empathize" with buyer personas, giving them a human form, a face and an identity. Therefore, we are talking about information such as age, sex, origin, level of education, employment and income, as well as data relating to marital status, the number of children and the family unit. It is no coincidence, then, that Meerman Scott recommends giving a name to the buyer personas, precisely because these types of data allow you to "humanize" your company and related marketing strategies. Establishing that, for example, we must turn to Jane, a 37-year-old woman from New York, with more than one child and happily married, is useful to make the image that professionals have of a specific target group less abstract. This will simplify and identify the correct way they must address the communication of the brand or product.

In some cases, it may also be crucial to know the skills of the customer or typical user of our site. For example, the development of the design of a site or software or the versions of a site in different languages may vary depending on the target who in fact may be particularly familiar with those tools or may instead be a beginner. The same thing is true for linguistic skills. You have to ask yourself if a specific target group on the site knows the English language or if it is necessary to create a version in other languages as well. This, in particular, is something to be taken into consideration very seriously, especially in this multiethnic world.

Psychographic data

To understand how a certain type of customer thinks, it is also necessary to carry out a psychographic analysis, taking up elements that make it possible to identify some personality traits, attitudes, ways of thinking and typical saying of a particular buyer persona. For example, it would be appropriate to understand if it is more or less extroverted, if it is impulsive (which can affect the type of purchases and the impact of advertising communications), if it is particularly emotional or more rational, if it is more or less tending to savings, etc.

In addition to the preponderant character traits, we must also ask ourselves what fears, anxieties or frustrations can be. Think of a company that produces toys and the importance of identifying the greatest concerns of parents for their children. This, however, is not enough because it is useful to understand what leads them to buy that product. For example, parents could aim to buy a more "educational" toy, asking for opinions in the store or doing online searches, while grandparents could aim to please the child, deciding to buy a toy advertised in a TV commercial, perhaps even more expensive but which can satisfy the grandson's requests. This information can be useful in making decisions regarding the characteristics of the product, the price, but also the tone of voice of the advertising messages, therefore depending on the buyer persona to whom it is addressed.

Another important aspect concerns the predominant system of values for each buyer persona, that is, what are the moral principles not to be infringed, what kind of communication or marketing action could go against the ethical principles of a specific type of consumer. In this regard, as many experts explained over the years, it is necessary to identify the values that our brand or our site must keep alive in order not to go against the moral values of the users to whom it is approaching. Why? because, if on the one hand we are quite inclined and available to a change of opinion on certain ideas or concepts when someone (such as a brand) tries to convince us of something, on the other hand there are certain principles or values to which we are not willing to give up. One thing is certain values do not change and, on the contrary, we feel a sense of disgust and anger towards those who try to transmit moral values that are different from ours. Discover the value of your ideal customers and build your social media marketing strategy on them.

Furthermore, it is necessary to take into account not only the values but also any prejudices or preconceptions, conventions and opinions that people have regarding the most varied topics that can in some way interfere with the evaluation of a product or an advertisement and must be identified. and taken into consideration.

Needs, motivations and objectives of the buyer personas

Knowing the motivations, priorities and needs that lead customers to seek a specific solution, to solve a problem, to find out about the different brands that offer a certain service or to buy a certain product is essential to know what to focus economic efforts on identify the elements or characteristics to be highlighted in the communication of a product or brand.

On Alan Cooper's website, Kim Goodwin mentions the different types of objectives or expectations of the buyer persona that should be identified and which must affect the design of sites, products and planning of marketing strategies. The expert refers above all to life goals, such as retiring at 45. This particular goal may not be of great relevance to anyone designing a phone, but it may be useful for someone who is creating a financial planning tool.

Limits, problems and barriers to purchase

Another important element to analyze in detail is the perception that customers have of the brand or its products. Knowing the preconceptions, opinions and criticisms that consumers have to move to a given solution will allow brands to respond accordingly, proposing changes based on the various problems identified. Furthermore, once any obstacles to purchase have been identified, that is, anything that could lead a customer to decide that they no longer want to buy the product or even try it, companies can create a communication that allows them to overcome these obstacles.

Decision criteria

What criteria do different customers or users focus on for purchasing decisions? Knowing what drives consumers to choose one brand to the detriment of another is of great importance for companies, since it allows you to understand not only what the advantages that make your product essential for a specific target are, but also the problems that make it so that it prefers the solution offered by a competitor.

Buyer journey

The analysis of the buyer journey is essential first of all to understand which are the points of contact with the company that will allow you to reach the customer effectively, inspiring trust and meeting the preferences for the use of content and research of the information. It is necessary to know the process or the path taken by customers before arriving at the purchase of the product, so as to understand what difficulties or problems there are and how to overcome them effectively.

It is therefore of great interest to obtain data on all the obstacles that can intervene in the purchase process. How can you do this? For example, you can achieve this by asking the user the type of sources they use when looking for information on products or services and through which channels they usually receive or would prefer to receive commercial communications. Remember, if you control the journey of your customer you control your customer.

Effective tools for data collection

There are several tools that allow you to collect the information needed to build buyer personas. Social media, and therefore tools such as Facebook Audience Insights but also Google Analytics, can be very useful for collecting large amounts of demographic data, as well as the times in which each group of users is most active on the web, their geographical origin and related interests.

In addition to the processing of statistical data relating to personal data or purchasing behavior, the carrying out of interviews is particularly important because it also allows you to analyze the type of language used by the buyer personas and therefore understand the style of communication, the words, the terms that may hit them more. Therefore, it may be useful to extract from these one or more representative quotes of each buyer persona, their motivations, fears, aspirations, expectations towards brands or products but also their life goals, for example. On the basis of this information, short bibliographic descriptions can be constructed that can serve as inspiration for the creation of content aimed at that specific group of customers. You can also use online surveys sent via email through, for example, Google Form.

How to analyze the data you collect

Once the data has been collected, how to put them together to create the identities of the ideal customer or the different types of customers? As for the ideal number of buyer personas, according to David Meerman Scott, it must be identified "on the basis of the factors that differentiate them".

For example, some companies may have a different profile to represent the Asian, European and North American customer, thus creating different archetypes according to the different geographical areas in which it operates. It all depends on the sector, the type of company and business you offer, as well as the different target groups involved.

Chapter 10 - Content Strategy: Everything You Need to Know

Content strategy and content marketing are often confused and used as synonyms, but they are and remain well-defined elements with the first being hierarchically superior to the second. In fact, we will see how a content strategy can exist without even a glimpse of content marketing. Because "content is king" remains a valid dogma, but there is no king without a kingdom that has precise borders within which to exercise its hegemony.

Before diving deeper into content marketing, it is important to give a definition of what we are talking about and distinguish content marketing from content strategy.

Content marketing - definition

Content marketing is the creation and dissemination of useful and valuable content, aimed at a well-defined audience, with the aim of attracting it, acquiring it and inducing potential customers to take profitable actions.

Content strategy - definition

Content strategy deals with the planning aspects of content management throughout its life cycle. It includes the analysis phase, the alignment of the content with the business goals, influencing its development, production, presentation, evaluation, measurement and archiving. What the content strategy is not, however, is the content implementation phase. Practical development, management and dissemination of content are the tactical results of the strategy, what needs to be done for the strategy to be effective.

Thus, Rahel Anne Bailie, a famous content strategis, in an article on her blog dated 2009 but still valuable, stated this exact difference.

Basically, the two phases are split. The first one involves strategic planning and the second one, which is subsequent and regulated by the first, involves the creation and share of the content in its different forms.

Content strategy is what lies upstream, it is the planning activity that defines and regulates this process. The difference lies in the fact that the content strategist does not deal with the production of content but turns his attention to the planning of the same, not limiting himself to defining when they should be published but above all why they should be produced. Each content, in fact, must be a single brick useful to build the bigger building. It is a work of engineering and architecture for which not only workers and concrete are needed, but first of all a clear, defined project divided into several phases. Without precise planning, clear goals to strive for and measurable objectives to be achieved, the contents will be ineffective and self-referential. They simply won't "stand up", exactly like a building built in the absence of a blueprint.

Content strategy and content curation

As evidence of how much and how the content strategy has an absolute value greater than content marketing, there are numerous examples of strategies of extraordinary success without even the production of their own content. In this case, we leverage on content curation (defined as the ability to filter and add value to the contents we receive daily from all online sources, i.e. the process of selection, collection, organization and subsequent sharing of content relating to a particular topic or subject area).

We can offer useful content to potential customers that are simultaneously in line with our business goals. We are referring to reporting, commenting and rewriting articles written by third parties that thus enter the information sphere of our audience. In this way, we will add a valuable contribution capable of underlining our expertise in the field, the relevance of the subject for our industry and the usefulness of that information for those who receive it.

Structuring a winning content strategy

In a broader marketing action, whether it is inbound marketing or social media marketing, content remains the main focus or at least it should. In defining the strategy, a good content strategist can and must make use of numerous tools and suggestions to identify topics of interest. Among these, in addition to what a paid platform like Hubspot offers, Google offers valuable and free help. Through the Adwords keyword planner it is possible to know the search volume for the keyword that has been identified as being of interest for the target audience. Google Trends, on the other hand, allows you to measure the degree of interest of that keyword in a given period, thus knowing its variations, noticing any new trends.

However, the choice of specific topics to be treated is a step subsequent to numerous others that precede it. It will be essential to first establish what the goals of our marketing action are and which target we would like to talk to. Subsequently it will be necessary to identify a message that differentiates us from the competition and that can be the beacon of our communication. Then, thoroughly analyze the market and competitors and identify the most suitable channels to spread our messages. Finally, establish what KPIs to measure to be aware of the progress of our strategy.

Defining the goals for your content strategy in the most effective way

A content strategist is called upon to confront the objectives indicated by the companies for which he works. Often, these milestones are rather vague, complicated to quantify.

"I would like to have more visibility". Would it mean having more visitors to your site? Or, "I would like to increase sales". Ok, but on which segments? Not having a magic strategy that works for everything, you need to choose which categories of people to focus your communication on to try to increase sales in that specific area. It is therefore necessary to discuss and define the goals in advance in a precise and specific way. It is on the basis of them, moreover, that each individual content and the entire content strategy must be oriented.

For example, "increasing sales generated from the youngest portion of our clients" could be a clear, concrete, measurable goal and referred to a specific target.

But what are the most common goals that a content strategy can aim to achieve? Here is an exhaustive list, that will give you a better idea on where to focus your attention.

• **Lead generation.** Contents and landing pages structured in such a way as to facilitate the compilation of a form through which to obtain useful information on potential customers.

• **Media and digital pr.** Our goal will be to obtain media coverage by creating news that has an organic, viral diffusion.

• **Distinctive positioning.** Our purpose will be defined by communicating what exactly the company does, positioning it precisely in that sector and distinguishing it from its competitors. This is an extremely important goal that, if achieved can lead to enormous amount of success.

• **Customer support.** Our contents will be aimed at clarifying the terms and conditions of the service, the characteristics of the products and the sales mechanisms.

- **Community building.** Our editorial plan will be aimed at creating a sense of belonging, identification towards the brand through a sharing of values that emerges from a story that is as shared as possible, horizontal, friendly.

The definition of the target of a content strategy: the buyer persona

As discussed in the previous chapter, identifying the correct buyer persona is extremely important in a social media marketing strategy.

Mapping the purchasing process and intervening at every stage with the right content, at the right time, aimed at the right person is the overall and final goal of a well rounded content strategy.

To understand if a message is interesting or not, if a content can be relevant or not, we will have to understand who should receive it. Have in mind who to turn to at every time, as this is a crucial part of every social media marketing strategy.

Identifying your audience, defining it as specifically as possible is the key to drawing up a winning content strategy. Information such as age, gender, educational qualification, for many product categories are now superfluous.

At all levels of marketing, a fall in the importance of personal data is being observed in favor of buyer personas. The modern identity of the potential customer we address is reconstructed by integrating demographic and, above all, psychographic data. This means taking into strong consideration interests, behaviors, reasons for purchasing, doubts and fears regarding our service, product or our entire industry.

In short, information that is not only useful but essential to understand in which contexts these categories of people are more accessible and inclined to listen to our message and what makes that message relevant for them. We will have a dedicated chapter on this topic later on in this book.

Identify the differential message of the content strategy

Differentiate to qualify, that is key. A winning content strategy cannot ignore the identification of a differential message, of a corporate plus value that allows us to stand out from the competition. Our differential message will be our beacon. In fact, in all our content we will have to ask ourselves if it has been underlined, or at least implied. And it must be one and only one. The customer is bombarded with numerous advertisements every time he logs in and is looking for someone who can simplify his choice by clarifying which is the best, or most immediate, for that need he wants to satisfy.

It is not enough to position yourself only for the characteristics of your product

It is necessary that these are also sought after by the market and that they are not already totally controlled by the competition. In other words, you have to trigger a need and the inability to satisfy it by your competitor. That is how you win in business.

Positioning yourself on the market for a certain category or quality allows you to differentiate yourself from others

The entire content strategy will be defined by always referring to the added value that we guarantee and will aim to associate the brand with that distinctive feature that allows the simplest and most immediate mental association possible for the final consumer.

Market and competition analysis

We know we want to differentiate ourselves, but how can we do it if we do not have full and precise knowledge of what our competitors are doing?

Content strategy is still marketing, and marketing needs a benchmark. A comparative analysis with respect to our direct competitors is essential to trace the differences, their respective weaknesses and strengths. Without forgetting a broader investigation than what other similar companies do but outside our specific market, in order to obtain some useful ideas to integrate our content marketing plan.

Multi-channel content strategy

A multi-channel content strategy is essential. Stories and contents on the internet can branch out expanding, wandering, deepening, even through hypertext links. They can migrate between multiple platforms, channels, also passing from online to offline and vice versa. Our final consumer himself is now multi-channel, therefore multiplying the possibilities of intercepting him can only be one of our primary objectives.

We will have to do this by taking into account that each channel has its own characteristics that define it, peculiarities that must be taken into account already in the strategy definition phase, devising contents that can intercept and engage the audience that uses them.

What works for Facebook will most likely not work for LinkedIn, or Twitter and vice versa. The people reached will be different, the communication model adopted on the different platforms will be different.

Ignoring this aspect and republishing the same content on each different digital channel can only condemn our editorial plan to irrelevance.

Organic share and promoted content

A good web content editor knows he has to follow the guides provided by the content strategist on the creation and dissemination of his contents. It will also be essential, already in the drafting phase of the strategy, to define a budget to be allocated to sponsored content. Entrusting your editorial calendar to organic distribution alone could be very limiting.

Social advertising allows us to define with extreme precision the audience we can hit. Furthermore, knowing right from the start on which categories of content to invest in order to guarantee them the necessary "push" to establish themselves and get closer to our business objectives simplifies and simplifies processes.

Chapter 11 - Content Strategies for Different Buyer Personas

In previous chapters we have discussed the importance of having a good content strategy. We have also touched on the point that there is not a better content in absolute terms, but that it depends on who consumes said content. Let's dive a bit deeper in this concept.

Creating customized content for different buyer personas is essential to engage different consumer or user groups. David Meerman Scott gives the example of the creation of a university site that must address buyer personas with very different characteristics, objectives and motivations. In this case, the site must contain pages with content suited to the needs and expectations of the various interested parties.

Demonstrating how the creation of content can vary within the same site, the expert illustrates five possible buyer personas to be developed: former students, who are contacted to convince them to make donations; high school students, worried about submitting an application for university access and who need clear and detailed information; the parents of prospective students, who will certainly look for reassuring information on where the off-site students will live; current students to be persuaded to enroll again in a master's or other course of study; a more general section with the most frequently asked questions to avoid wasting time in university offices.

Different people come to the site or shop for different reasons, they are used to a different language and expect to find a certain type of information or certain products, which is why marketers, as explained by the expert, should undertake to use the information on buyer personas to create specific marketing and PR plans to reach each one of them.

Chapter 12 - Facebook: a Basic Introduction

Facebook Marketing is a complex topic that encompasses different functionalities, strategies, tools and features for each company and type of business. In this section, we are going to discuss every aspect there is to know to turn your Facebook page into a money making machine.

Whether you are a small local merchant, a restaurant or store, a multinational brand, on Facebook you will find tools that can help you improve your visibility, build a community, increase the awareness of your brand and the sales of your product or service, online and offline.

Facebook Marketing is a constantly evolving topic. In fact, the social media constantly updates the tools made available to companies, adding new features and expanding its capabilities.

Facebook in the US is now known and used by almost 300 million people, so it is useless to explain what the functionalities of a basic profile are, we know them very well and this book is all about giving you the most valuable information.

What no many people know and what we are going to focus on, instead, is the importance that Facebook has assumed as the best social media marketing and social e-commerce platform in the entire world.

In this section we will address the main topics of facebook marketing. You will discover the bases for a successful social media strategy. You will learn how to do facebook marketing and how to use social marketing to increase your facebook business by managing facebook fan pages and facebook ads.

Finally, we will offer you some examples of facebook social media marketing, reporting the success stories of the best brands present online. Finally, you will have all the basic information to build your winning Facebook marketing strategies and be able to plan your social media manager training in the most effective way, if this is the route you want to take.

To start making the most of this social network by promoting your website or blog and increasing your online business, it is essential to define the goal we want to achieve. These can be:

● Promote our Brand (brand awareness)

- Build a user base
- Increase visits to the site or to individual blog articles
- Promote the sale of a product or service
- Provide a stellar customer service

Once the goals have been defined, it will be useful to create a Facebook company profile or public profile that allows a relationship between company and user.

First of all, this will be useful because you can start the dialogue with your fans, users and potential customers. Furthermore, you will then be able to use paid advertising to monetize this first audience even further.

Let's start by understanding the difference between a company page and a personal profile. When we are talking about a business page, users can decide to become followers of the company but not "friends" as happens by sending a request from a private profile.

Fans will be able to comment and express appreciation for the links and share them with their friends, creating a viral marketing mechanism. However, it will then be necessary to profile users based on interests, in fact the facebook page could reach thousands of fans but not all of them interested in the proposed contents.

So, what should you use? No matter if you have a personal brand or a multinational company. If you want to use Facebook in a professional way, always choose a business page over a personal profile. In fact, you will not be able to run ads on a personal profile, which is a big disadvantage.

Before understanding how Facebook Marketing works, let's try to explain the main fundamentals and some key concepts that characterize this social network.

Network of friendship

Facebook is based on developing and maintaining its network of online friendships. To contact a person you would like to be part of your network, you need to send a friend request. It is easily done via a button called Add to friends. In this way, you will be able to get in touch with another registered person like you: think of an old school friend you haven't seen in a long time that you found in the search engine once you have typed in his name and surname.

Likes and comments

The like key is undoubtedly, together with the comments key, one of the most popular functions of Facebook. The thumbs up expresses appreciation for a post, a photo, opinion and video on Facebook, thus allowing interaction. By clicking on the comments button users can publish your opinion on a content and make it visible to others.

Sharing

Thanks to this feature it is possible to share the contents of a page you follow, the update of personal status or of your contact, a video, a photo that you think are also interesting for other people. If you can get a lot of people to share your company posts, you are doing very well.

Notifications

The notification is that red square to report a new update, message and contact request. If you can manage to appear in the notification section of your potential clients, you are in a great position as you will surely catch their attention.

Status update

At the top of the profile home you can write a personal status that you want to share with your friends or fans. This is an important feature to share content with your audience and it is where most of your content strategy should take place.

Tag

It is a mention that a contact makes of another through a text that shows the exact name and surname of the person tagged. You can be mentioned on a photo or in a post and the recipient is notified by a notification. Tagging brands you will collaborate with is a great strategy to create a virtuous cycle of engagement.

Chat

Thanks to the chat two contacts can exchange unlimited messages in private mode. You can do this quickly by clicking on the message icon at the top, select the person and start a conversation. Thanks to the Facebook Messenger application you can do it easily even via your mobile phone. It has been more and more common to use chatbot in a social media marketing strategy to communicate directly with your potential customers.

Now that we have discussed the very basic concept of Facebook, it is time to see how you can use it to actively increase your brand exposure and reach more potential customers. We will start by taking a look at how to properly structure a business page.

Chapter 13 - How to Correctly Structure a Facebook Page for your Business or Personal Brand

Now that we have learned about the basics of Facebook, it is time to take a look at how to correctly set up a business page. This is a crucial step, as it will allow you to run paid ads to your page, creating engagement with your target audience and helping your brand to get noticed. Let's see how to set up the page.

The first thing you need to know is that the creation of a Facebook page can be done directly through the official website of the social network or through the Facebook application available for free on smartphones and tablets.

In both cases, all you need to create a Facebook page is a personal profile on the well-known social network platform, as to proceed with the creation of a Facebook page the first thing you will have to do is log in to Facebook with your profile to then follow the instructions we are about to give you step by step.

You must also know that Facebook pages are created and managed by administrators. Administrators are nothing more than people in charge of proceeding with the creation and management of a company page in all of its aspects. In essence, therefore, if you have been instructed by your company to carry out this operation, you will need to keep in mind that the company Facebook page must be created and managed through your personal account.

Do not worry, your private information, such as your name, surname or email address, will not be displayed on the Facebook page created. In essence, you can have as many pages as you want, without other people knowing you are the administrator.

Having clarified these fundamental issues, let's get to the heart of the matter. To create a Facebook page, after logging into your profile, go to the official Facebook for Business website and press the "Create a page" button that you can see in the top right corner.

Once you click on the Create a Page button, you will be redirected to the initial section dedicated to creating a Facebook page. You will then have to choose the Company or brand option, by clicking on the relevant Start button, and follow the instructions on the screen to complete the procedure for creating your page.

You must therefore type the name of the page and the category to which it belongs in the text fields that are proposed to you. To indicate the category (e.g. website or retail company), you need to start typing a term and then select one of the suggestions that appear below. When completed, click on the "Continue" button to go on.

Now choose whether to upload a profile picture for the page (by clicking on the appropriate button) or whether to skip the step. Then repeat the same operation for the cover image and that's it. You will be automatically redirected to the main section of your new page, through which you can manage all the contents of the same. We will discuss what kind of images to use on your brand's social pages in a later chapter. If you are following along, you can skip this step for now.

To make your page more complete, you need to enter all the information related to it. Click the button under the cover image, select the Edit page information item from the menu that opens and fill out the form that is proposed to you with information such as telephone number, reference website, position geographical etc.

Remember that the more complete your page profile is, the more reliability you will communicate to your audience.

We recommend creating all your pages using a laptop, as it is much easier and faster. However, you can do this using your smartphone or tablet as well. In this case, things are a little different. Here is how to do it.

How to create a Facebook page using the Facebook app

If you want to create a company Facebook page from mobile devices, you must install the official Facebook application for Android, iOS or Windows 10 Mobile. If you don't know how to do it, read my guide dedicated to the topic.

Once installation is complete, log into your account and press the ☰ button (which is located at the bottom right on iOS and at the top right on Android). Then select the item Pages from the screen that opens, press the + Create button (on Android) or the Create a page item (on iOS) and press the Start button.

Now, type the name you want to assign to your page in the appropriate text field, press the "Next" button and select a category from the appropriate drop-down menu (e.g. Brand and products or local businesses), then a subcategory from the menu that appears at the bottom and press the "Next" button again.

In the screen that appears later, type the address of the website referring to the page and click "Next". If you do not want to enter any website, tap on the "Skip" button located at the top right of your screen. Finally, choose whether to add a profile picture and a cover image for the page and, if so, select a photo from your device. Alternatively, press the "Skip" button to bypass the procedure. You can change the profile picture and the cover image at any time.

The game is done! Now press the "Visit the page" button to view your page and follow the advice you find in the Basic Elements box for the new Pages to add all the information relating to the latter.

To view the complete list of information that can be entered on the page and fill in the appropriate forms, scroll through the tabs located under the buttons for publishing content, choose the "Information" tab and tap on the "Edit information" button on the page that appears at the bottom of your screen.

Chapter 14 - Choose the Best Images for your Facebook Page

If you think that the Facebook cover image is just a simple photo to embellish your page, you are wrong. This image can in fact represent a springboard for your brand or for your company, even more so now that the new page layout announced by Facebook will give greater visibility to the creativity and message placed in this section.

The cover image is the perfect space to tell those who visit your profile something more about your brand and your products, but above all it is the perfect space to encourage a call-to-action, which can be a purchase on your ecommerce, a visit to your physical store or a phone call for a quote request.

To improve the effectiveness of your company Facebook page, first try to follow these small technical tips:

- Make sure the image dimensions are correct. The old Facebook pages required an image of 851 pixels wide and 315 pixels high; the new ones with 2021 layout require images 1014 pixels × 384 px;

- Use visual or textual elements that focus attention;

- Make your cover image an integral part of your marketing strategy;

- Upload new images on a constant basis and use the space to highlight news, promotions and initiatives of your business (giveaways, events, new products);

- Update (or try to) your cover at least once a month;

- Use the visual element to answer the visitor's hypothetical question "why should I like this page?".

This list, in addition to being already useful, can however be supplemented by 12 other creative ways to use the cover image of your Facebook page to make what you do, your company or your products, more visible and attractive.

So let's dive deeper into this topic and discover everything there is to know about choosing the perfect image for your Facebook page.

1) Inspire customers to buy your products

Surely you know how videos are very useful tools to explain to people how to take advantage of a product or service.

The same opportunity can be exploited through photos.

In fact, when you showcase what you do in your cover image, you are planting ideas in the minds of your potential customers, which could lead them to contact you to buy your product or choose your service.

In its cover image, Edible Arrangements (a company specialized in fruit compositions for events) has put its product at the center and at the forefront with a "happy birthday" message in the background, to highlight how its products are a great idea good for a gift or for decorations for a birthday party.

It's a very subtle tactic, but you can use it to portray your brand by stating "my product is something special" or "my product may be what you are looking for to give something special".

2) Show off what you do

Are you able to explain what your company does in just a second?

One of the best ways to spice up your cover image is to come up with creative ideas to advertise what you do in a way that informs people who find your brand on Facebook at a glance.

This is exactly what EYStudios (an eCommerce design company) did with its new cover image: a sharp and impactful photo that undoubtedly shows who the company is and what it does.

3) Express your personality

Visual content is a very important part of your marketing and is the best way to show who you are and what personality is behind your work.

The cover of the company Facebook page is the perfect showcase to insert an image in line with the message that the company wants to convey beyond Facebook.

MailChimp, for example, uses his photo to show who the company is and his personality, using empty spaces to highlight the main subject of the photo, in order to attract all attention to it.

4) Appeal to the senses

Companies in the food sector have the opportunity to capture attention by using tempting photos of their products so as to make the observer's mouth water.

These companies have the ability to update the cover image very often both to highlight what the menu offers and to highlight any promotions.

The cover of the Facebook business page of Little Caesars (the third largest pizza chain in the US) is a blatant example of this tactic.

Papa John's (another major company in the sector) followed the same path by highlighting the product with the promotion of the moment, while also leaving some space to underline its relationship with the Major League of Baseball.

If you are aware of the fact that your customers have specific preferences regarding some of your products, you can use this information to appeal to customers even more.

This is what the Olive Garden chain of restaurants has done. Since the company is aware that the most popular products are breadsticks and huge salads, it showed them in the foreground in the cover image and photographed them so closely that it almost seems to be sitting at the table. Cruel, but effective.

5) Contact a circle of users

For specific product companies, the Facebook cover image is the perfect way to represent not only new and upcoming products but also the latest promotions.

To maximize the impact, it is certainly effective to insert a compelling reproduction of the product, information on it, release dates in stores and "call to action".

Logitech G, a PC accessories company, used its cover image to promote a specific product line.

The company took advantage of the space to emphasize its link with the ESL (Internet Sports League) to promote products for players.

6) Inspire creativity

Your Facebook cover doesn't always have to be the place for notifications and promotions. Often the message you want to send can get through more effectively if creativity takes over.

Take a cue from the Toys "R" Us, a children related product company. The company has in fact used a photo that recalls both adults and children to play and imagination. Fun can sometimes come from the simplest of things.

7) Promote your hashtag

Hashtags are powerful marketing tools, as we have discussed in the introductory chapter to Facebook.

Many companies have had great success using them in marketing strategies, since with hashtags they have been able to monitor what users said about their products to improve them.

Give hashtags plenty of space on your cover image to ensure as much exposure as possible, as did Calvin Klein and Monster Energy.

By taking advantage of the Facebook page cover image to highlight your hashtags for each of your advertising campaigns, people will often start looking at your image in search of promotions and alerts.

8) Value your fans

To celebrate its 100th birthday, Oreo released a new cover image showing fans on their birthday.

Customers love being part of the brand's history. If you involve your fans you will make them feel valued, you will show authenticity and humanity as integral values of your company.

Red Bull is a leader in doing this: it loves inserting user-created content in its social media pages.

9) Play on emotions

Emotions play a fundamental role in how users will react to a product; the sensations that your products generate will therefore have a big impact.

Your cover image must exude emotions since it is these that guide decisions, changes of opinion, user requests.

Emotions are the best tool for strengthening customers' bond with a brand.

David's Bridal (a brand specializing in wedding planning) plays on the powerful emotions of couples, focusing especially on brides.

What it paints with her cover image is a scenario that generates emotion in the audience: it's the big day, you're married, the stress of the preparations is over and everything is perfect as you always dreamed.

Think back to the first time you went to the zoo. Each animal was a surprising discovery.

The Detroit Zoo through its cover image wants to remind you of that feeling and wants you to dive back into that memory.

The cover image of Parent Magazine, on the other hand, generates emotions related to being a parent with the aim of making readers feel almost understood. It is in fact a photo that makes people exclaim: "Parent Magazine knows what it means to be parents!"

10) Promote what your target audience likes

Companies that previously limited themselves to selling products, today attract customers with extensions of their businesses: entertainment, workshops, social experiments and much more.

Companies can therefore benefit greatly from promoting their products on Facebook. But it doesn't stop there.

Think about how your customers use your products or services and what part of those products remain most impressed.

Turn everything into a visual experience and insert it at the top of your Facebook page so that your followers will want to try it.

Great Wolf Lodge (a company specialized in water parks) is one example.

Of course, showing some nice photos of their water park would already have been effective, but showing the image of the giant water funnel is certainly more impactful.

Would you like to try it, right?

Polaris sells vehicles suitable for all types of terrain. The company knows very well how its products are actually used. It is crucial to know how your customers use your products and services.

11) Promote giveaways

There are many ways to notify your followers when you are about to start a giveaway. You can use push notifications, emails, flyers or simple word of mouth. However, many of these methods only reach those who already follow you.

Using the cover image instead allows you to make the content you want to advertise visible to all, especially new visitors.

KOA (a camping company), for example, is renowned for its large number of giveaways, which sometimes even include real caravans.

The cover image can therefore help visitors to always be aware of these giveaways. People like this will want to always be up to date on you.

12) Advertise your other social pages

If you want to have more followers on other social networks you need to let people know about them.

Use your Facebook cover image to let your users know that you have other social accounts so they can choose where and how to follow you!

Family-friendly comedian Batdad uses his cover image to showcase his other social channels and got enormous engagement on other platforms as well, thanks to this tactic.

As you can see, there is much more to choosing the perfect images for your Facebook page than "just choosing an image". Keep this in mind when you formulate the content strategy for your brand, as it can make or break the impact you have on your target audience.

Also, do not forget about the importance of colours. Each brand has to have its own colours, as they are a powerful vehicle to be recognized by the targeted audience. When you choose the colours for your brand, try to think about the idea and message you want to convey. For instance, if you are in the wellness niche, focus on light colours, as they communicate purity and well-being. On the contrary, if you operate in the "make money online" niche, you would like to focus on gold-like colours, conveying a message of abundance to your potential customers.

When it comes to social media marketing, everything is done for a reason and has a goal in mind, even the profile picture of your Facebook page. Do not forget it.

Chapter 15 - What to Do With a Business Facebook Page

Now that you have successfully learned how to create and correctly set up your Facebook page, it is time to discuss how to apply your content strategy in the best way possible. In this chapter, we are going to cover every tool at your disposal to make sure you maximize the power of your company Facebook page. Let's get started.

Every social media strategy on the web must combine quality content with a strategy capable of conveying the right message to the right people, at the right time. In this difficult strategic process, Facebook helps companies to advertise online, allowing them to create different, engaging content each time, capable of achieving multiple objectives, targeting them to specific targets.

Companies that want to promote online will obviously have to have a company Facebook profile. Therefore, the strategy to be adopted to convey the right message to the public will be planned. Facebook provides 10 different types of content or posts.

Here we explain in detail the differences between the 10 types of posts, with some useful tips to use them in the right way.

1. **Share a photo or video**

    You can share one or more photos, which you can also combine into an album, which will remain accessible to users within your company Facebook page. Together with the photo or post you can insert descriptive text, add emoticons with which you describe your mood, register your position in a specific place, perhaps your company headquarters, or another location if, for example, you are attending a corporate event. Finally, in the post you can also tag a product that is relevant to your brand. The use of posts with images and videos statistically have a much greater engagement than posts with text only, so you should prefer this type of post. Whenever possible, include the link to your business website in your post. In this way you will increase visits to the site.

1. **Advertise your company**

   With this method you can create sponsored posts that advertise your web page or your Facebook business page. Sponsored posts can be of various types: carousel, single image, link to the website, video and much more. The goals of the posts also may vary. You can choose whether to increase visits to the website, get more Likes on the Facebook page, increase the installations of your company app; in other words, you choose the goal and Facebook will help you achieve it. With the professional Facebook Ads Management tool, you can create effective promotions by monitoring their progress, target and budget. We will discuss more about Facebook ads in a dedicated chapter.

2. **Create an offer**

This feature allows you to create an offer, discount or promotion for your products. You will be able to include a special promotional code and also add conditions of sale. The promotion will include a photo, an expiration date and the remaining time. This is a very useful feature for promotions to be used on holidays or special occasions. Users can decide whether to save the offer, by receiving a notification before its expiration. This feature works seamlessly with the Facebook Showcase feature and is used by many users.

1. **Record a live video for your target audience**

If you have a camera and have a specific message to convey, this is the perfect function for you. The tool is widely used by those who work in the entertainment and art sectors. We advise you to plan its use and use it only if you are at corporate events that deserve attention, or if you have already prepared your audience with an announcement about the live broadcast. Communicate the live video topic first, as this is going to set the stage for a proper conversation with your audience. Ask your audience questions and ask them what they would like to question you about. During the live broadcast you will be able to interact with the connected audience, who will be able to comment via streaming messages. Over the years, this has become a very important tool for small and medium size companies and we advise you to use it extensively to increase brand awareness.

1. Receive phone calls from your customers or potential client

With this tool you will create a post with an upper writing, a lower image and a slogan under the image. At the bottom right, the user will find a button that reads "Call now". By clicking on it from their mobile phone your audience can directly call the number you entered. This is a very useful function if the call to action you want to get is the conversion through phone calls.

1. Receive messages

It is a post similar to the one listed above in point 5, except that instead of the "Call now" button, the user will find the "Send a message" button. This is a very useful new feature for companies, which may decide to invest in sponsored posts with this effective call to action. Users will feel pressured to send a private message via Facebook messenger. An instrument that is really popular nowadays.

1. Help people find your company

This new type of post consists of an initial text, an image, a slogan and a button with a call to action called "Directions". By clicking on that button, the user will be directed to a map with directions to reach your company headquarters. This is a particularly interesting feature if you have a physical store that you would like to bring customers to.

1. Create an event

A much more attractive tool since it contains the new feature that allows you to insert a video on the cover instead of the photo. Below you will enter the name of the event, the place, the frequency, the start and end date, the details, the keywords, the tickets and the URL to get the tickets. This tool is widely used in the world of art and music, to promote concerts and national premieres. It can also be used to advertise corporate events or training courses.

1. **Write a note**

This is a special tool to use as an alternative to the standard post when you have particular concepts or content to transmit, such as poems or long texts. The tab allows you to write a bit like you do in a blog, complete with a title, anchor text, italics, bold and much more. You can include an image and even a link to your company's website.

1. **Create a product**

This is an innovative tool that allows you to insert a photo or video, the name of the product, the price, the ability to put it on sale, the description and the ability to share the product on your page. You can also choose whether to make it visible to everyone or keep it private to a select audience.

Especially if you have a digital product, showcasing it on your Facebook page will be fundamental to increase the perception of your brand and to attract new customers.

Now that you know every tool at your disposal to share your content on your Facebook page, it is time to dive deeper into the most important aspect of using Facebook in a social media marketing strategy. We are talking about Facebook ads and the next chapter will tell you all about them.

Chapter 16 - Facebook Ads

Now that we have laid out the basics of Facebook for business, it is time to dive deeper into the most discussed and controversial topic regarding this social network. We are talking about the possibility to advertise, reaching potential customers and users by paying.

As always, let's start with a definition.

Defining Facebook ADS is pretty simple. It's Facebook's advertising system. ADS in fact stands for advertising, so the concept is quite clear. On how things work, things get a little more complicated, because if it is true that creating an ad is in itself a quick and painless process, creating an ad that achieves good or excellent results is pretty complex and requires a good dose of technical knowledge and experience.

But let's go step by step. Why should a company advertise on Facebook?

Given that later we will discuss in detail the specific goals that we can try to pursue thanks to Facebook ADS, in a nutshell we can now tell you that using this tool you have the possibility to propose your content or products to a group of potentially interested people; and you can do it by crossing the limit of fans of your fanpage, or by addressing a small subset of all subscribers.

Fan? fanpage? Yes, Facebook ADS is reserved for fan pages, you cannot start a campaign from your personal profile or from a group. And this explains the main reason why there is no point in trying to represent your business with anything other than a fanpage, as we have told you in previous chapters.

The reasons for the success of Facebook ADS

Why is Facebook ADS so talked about? The reason is actually very simple: it works very well. Over the course of its existence - that is, from the now distant 2011 until today - the Facebook advertising platform has undergone numerous updates, changes and second thoughts. The only aspect that has really remained unchanged is its performance. Obviously you must know how to move within the interface as well as you must necessarily know the concepts and variables that determine the success of a campaign. In this guide we will explain everything you need to know to start experimenting with this tool. The commitment and experience that you will accumulate by playing with Facebook ADS will do the rest. As for anything in life, practice makes perfect.

The structure of Facebook ADS campaigns

Regardless of the goal you choose, each Facebook ADS advertising campaign will be hierarchically structured on three distinct levels:

- **Level 1: Campaign** - In this first step you have to decide what will be the main goal that your ads will try to pursue. Once you have given a unique identifying name to the new campaign you can move on to the next level.

- **Level 2: Ad Group** - If the previous step was rather mechanical, here you will have to work more than that by defining the duration, the assigned budget and the target audience that will be reached by your ads. You will also decide on the placement and payment methods. It is important to note that a single campaign can contain multiple ad groups.

- **Level 3: Ads** - In this last step you will have to create the actual ad, or choose what users will see every time your ad is actually published on Facebook. Basically it is about creating posts by carefully choosing the copy (the portions of text that will make up the ad) and the visual (therefore images, videos or slideshows). Also in this case you must always keep in mind that a single group of advertisements can contain more than one ad.

Only three steps and yet - as we will see - the difficulties behind each of these are not to be underestimated. Knowing how to untangle this process will make the difference between a successful campaign and one that simply burns money unnecessarily. For the moment, however, let's worry about summarizing the structure of Facebook campaigns.

How to create a new Facebook ADS campaign

To create your first Facebook ADS campaign, start by clicking on the arrow found on any Facebook screen at the top right. From the drop-down menu that will be generated, press "Create ad".

As you can see we are ready to start. But first note that if you have some ad blocking extension installed on your browser (AdBlock Plus for example) you will receive an error message. To use Facebook ADS correctly, you will need to disable the blocks on Facebook domains or, alternatively, suspend the operation of the advertisement during the creation process.

The goals of Facebook ADS campaigns

As you can see, the goals available for Facebook ADS campaigns are numerous. Ten to be exact. They are all specific and each has its own unique features. All of them are perfect to meet a specific need your company or personal brand may have. However, for beginners, they can create a bit of confusion. Is it better to choose Increase conversions on your website or Drive people to your website? Better to highlight a post or promote the page? To answer these questions, we will describe each of these ten goals to you, but you too have to go all in with us to clear your mind.

Facebook Advertising must always be part of a well-defined online marketing strategy before attempting to create campaigns. We have discussed this many times when we talked about having a social media marketing strategy.

So in a certain way you should have set the goal before starting the ad creation process, this is not the moment to improvise. Now it is just a matter of putting into practice what you and your co-workers previously planned. I insist on this point because, on the contrary, most novice entrepreneurs with online marketing approach Facebook ads without adequate preparation. They think that after all it would be nice to find new customers and they throw themselves into the instrument without having clear their purposes and, in the most tragic cases, not even the nature of the medium. So always remember to plan before putting into practice!

Let's take a look at the different goals your campaign can have.

Direct people to your website

In this case, the goal of the campaign is to encourage users to click on the ad in order to view a page of your website. Once this goal has been selected, in fact, you will be asked to enter the URL of the page you want to promote.

Specify the address and you will be asked to create your Facebook Pixel. To do this, simply click on Create pixel and thanks to this Facebook will be able to optimize the performance of your campaigns. We will talk about the pixel in the next chapter. Once you have assigned a name to the new campaign, click on Create advertising account (if this is your first time in advertising on Facebook) or on Set audience and budget if you have already used Facebook ADS before.

Increase conversions on your website

In this case, the goal is to bring people to your website and, in addition, make them complete a purchase or a registration process. Conversion must therefore be interpreted with its broadest meaning, i.e. independent of the concept of sale.

To create a campaign of this type, you need to create a conversion pixel and install it correctly on the pages of your website. So, if you don't know how to create it and install it on your website, we invite you to read the next chapter, as it will explain everything you have to know about this topic.

Once the pixel has been created, you will need to specify a web address to promote and select a conversion action that signals Facebook that your goal has been achieved.

Why can't I just use the "Direct people to your website" feature?

Earlier we were talking to you about possible confusion between the various goals and now this question will probably whirl through your head. In this case and to an inexperienced eye, there could be an overlap between the two lenses. In reality this is not the case, of course. A campaign that targets conversions will choose to show ads to all people in the target audience that are similar to those who have completed a conversion in the past. While the goal of the campaign is to direct people to the website, the Facebook algorithm will look for people, among those who make up the target, particularly inclined to consult content shared on the social network. This will significantly reduce the cost of the campaign.

Make your posts stand out

With this aim, we are no longer trying to take people out of Facebook. Or at least this is not the main goal of this type of advertising. In this case we are trying to get engagement, meaning likes, comments and shares for a post that we have published on the page.

First, Facebook asks us to enter the name of the fanpage affected by the campaign or, if it is not possible to select it using the name, enter the URL of the same page. Obviously, in order to create an advertisement on behalf of a fanpage, it is necessary to have a suitable role in managing it.

After choosing the fanpage, you will be asked to indicate which post to highlight.

Increase participation in your event

If you have created an event from the manager of your fanpage and you want to ensure that potentially interested people in your area are aware of it, this is the type of campaign for you. As with the previous goals, just enter the name or address of the event to be promoted to begin the creation process.

Get people to ask for your offer

Practically the exact copy of the previous goal, but in this case we will highlight an offer. Note, however, that what is here understood as an offer is not a promotion or discount on your website, but an offer created using the appropriate publication tool on the fan pages.

Get video views

If you have published native videos on Facebook and want to increase their views, this type of campaign is ideal for achieving your goal. Also in this case a useful clarification is needed. As you can see, we specified native videos, that is, uploaded directly to Facebook. You can't use this feature to promote content posted on YouTube, Vimeo, or other video sharing platforms. In these cases, if you need to increase their visibility through Facebook ADS, you will need to create an ad hoc post on your fanpage and sponsor them using the "Highlight your posts" goal.

But what difference does it make?

As in the previous cases, here too it is a question of target audience optimization. In the case of featured posts, we seek engagement for certain types of posts. Regarding video views, Facebook will focus on selecting people who have shown particular interest in videos and perhaps who tend to see them for longer than others.

Now that we have seen the main goals you can choose from when creating a campaign, it is time to focus on the actual creation process.

Creating an advertising account

If this is your first time using Facebook ADS, after selecting the campaign goal and filling in all the required fields, you will have clicked on the "Create advertising account" button.

In the advanced settings you will be given the option to change the name of the account which, without changes, will take the name of your Facebook profile. Once we have checked that all settings are correct, we can proceed to the next step.

Ad groups

Well, now that you have selected the goal of your new campaign, Facebook wants to know other essential information: who to show your ads to, the period within the advertising campaign will be active and what your spending budget is.

In order to avoid turning the reading of this chapter into a too extreme test of mental resilience, we cannot show you the creation of ad groups and, subsequently, the ads for each different campaign seen previously. Each will have its own configuration details, but what is really important in a beginner's guide, as this one, are the general concepts and these will be addressed in great detail.

Definition of the target audience

It all starts here and believe us when we tell you that this is the most delicate step of the whole creative process. Later you will understand why, for the moment, trust us and pay a lot of attention.

We must skim and try to reduce the potential audience in order to isolate all those who might be genuinely interested in what we have to propose.

To keep track of the number of people who make up your audience and an estimate of the quality of your targeting, you will find a graph and an indication of the potential coverage of the ad group in the top right. As for the graph, always keep in mind that it is more choreographic and is able to correctly report only the extreme cases, so do not rely too much on it.

In order to select the proper audience, you have to have your buyer persona in mind. This is why it is extremely important that you do the research process described in the previous chapters, before creating your first ad. This will take a bit of time, but it will save you a lot of money.

Why don't we show the ad to everyone instead? isn't it cheaper?

No, it is a mentality that, although it might be right in some areas, is exactly the opposite of that required to be successful with Facebook Advertising. The algorithm that determines how much we will pay for achieving individual goals - in this case how much we will pay each time a user clicks on the ad and reaches the website - depends on how often the people to whom the ads are shown perform that particular action. In jargon we call it "Click Through Rate" (CTR) and it is expressed as a percentage.

If an ad is shown 100 times receiving 5 clicks, the corresponding CTR will be 5%. Although in reality the factors that come into play to determine the cost of each action are many, as an approximation we can safely assert that the "Cost Per Action" (CPA) is indirectly proportional to the CTR, so the more the percentage of people who click on the content increases, the more the CPA decreases.

Going back to the definition of the audience, you should now have clearer why it is so important. In fact, if we show our advertisement to a selected group of people so that many of them are interested, we will get a high CTR thus lowering the CPA. By maintaining an extremely large and heterogeneous audience, the CTR will inevitably plummet, sending the CPA sky high.

Why did Facebook do this devilry?

One of Facebook's goals has always been to avoid the invasion of traditional advertising on its pages. When the introduction of an advertising system became necessary to capitalize on the enormous volume of subscriptions, they set themselves the goal of programming an algorithm that would allow users to be reached only by quality content and in which they could be really interested. In this way, advertising stops being invasive and, on the contrary, can even become useful for discovering products and services that we are not aware of.

It is a sort of transparent advertising, therefore, which in order to be realized needs the collaboration of all advertisers. Clearly we could not expect a free collaboration and this payment system has proved to be the best deterrent for the incapable advertisers, since, in addition to spending more on average, a poorly performing ad will tend to be delivered more rarely by Facebook and therefore will reach a increasingly fewer number of users at the same cost. In short: it is not convenient at all to target everyone on the planet.

Now that we understand that targeting your ad audience is very important, it's time to go into detail and see how to properly define it. Please, keep in mind that you should have a specific idea of your target before starting the ad creation process.

Demographic targeting

In the first section we can affect purely demographic parameters. The preset location is the US, but we can select any place, even the smallest villages. When a municipality is selected, Facebook allows us to establish a radius in addition to the city within which to show the ad.

By acting on the selector next to the number of kilometers, we can narrow or expand the area involved.

At the moment all people who are in the area are selected. So a passing tourist stopped at a motorway restaurant could see our ad if he uses Facebook, perhaps from a smartphone. However, we can change this type of setting by acting on the selector at the top, or on the button on which you find written "All the people in this place".

There are four possible settings:

- All people in this place: will involve everyone who access Facebook in the demarcated area for the ad group.

- People who live in this place: it will involve all users who have reported the residence within the set range of action.

- People who were recently in this place: it will involve all the people who recently passed through the selected area.

- People traveling to this place: it will involve all people whose most recent position is the selected area based on the information provided by the mobile device.

It is also important to note that, again in terms of geographical delimitation, we can include and exclude other locations. By clicking on "Include" we will open a drop-down menu from which to select the option that allows us to choose other areas to exclude and include.

Age, gender and language

After specifying the area of action of our advertising group, we can proceed by defining the age, gender and language spoken by the people interested in our advertisement. The language field is particularly important and should not be confused with the area of residence: imagine in fact that you want to offer Italian language courses. Obviously you will try to select people living in Italy who have not set Italian as their main language.

Detailed targeting

Here we go straight to the heart of targeting. Through the detailed targeting fields we can in fact specify the interests and behaviors of the people we are going to reach. If you start typing something, Facebook will take care to give you some suggestions. In any case, you will have to select the characteristics that best describe the interested public, thus delimiting the potential coverage of the ad group.

To successfully accomplish this task we can use:

- Demographics
- Interests
- Behaviors
- Other categories

To go into more detail, you can start typing and see the suggestions offered by the interface or use the Browse tab and navigate between the various categories.

Before proceeding with the creation of your campaign, we advise you to carefully browse the categories in order to realize the real potential of the tool.

Exclude people or narrow your audience

So far we have entered interests or behaviors and we have broadened the target audience. In fact, the interests indicated so far are linked through a logical disjunction, namely:

Public = Interest1 or Interest2 or Interest3 or... or Interest4

If, on the other hand, you want to restrict the audience by cutting off people you do not think may be interested, you have two features available.

- Exclude People. It allows you to select interests, behaviors or demographics in the same ways you used previously. However now you are not adding but excluding people who match the selected characteristics. If you add more than one, a user just needs to meet at least one of the listed criteria to be excluded.

- Narrow the audience. Again you will select the interested audience by indicating the characteristics as done previously. However, now you are asking Facebook's algorithm to compose the audience so that, in addition to all the other characteristics, users also satisfy at least one of those indicated here.

Please note that you are not obliged to use all the targeting possibilities offered. However, especially by keeping in mind what has been said about the relationship between CTR and CPA, we invite you to think carefully when you are going to create your audiences in order to make the best possible use of the tools you have available.

The connections

To complete the definition of the target audience for your new Facebook Ads campaign, only the last piece is missing: connections. Thanks to these, you can further define your selection by adding or excluding people based on how they previously came in contact with your online business.

Connections allow you to target based on different types of actions they have performed so far. In detail:

Facebook pages

- People who like your page
- Friends of people who like your page
- Exclude people who like your page

Applications

- People who have used your application
- Friends of people who have used your application
- Exclude people who have used your application

Events

- People who responded to your event
- Friends of the people who responded to your event
- Exclude people who have already responded to your event

Therefore, supposing you want to create a new campaign to increase the likes of your company's fanpage, obviously you will want to exclude people who already like your page so as not to show your ad unnecessarily and thus trigger the usual vicious circle between CTR and CPA.

If you notice using this type of selection it is not possible for you to intersect the various results. For example, you can't target everyone who has used your application while excluding people who are fans of your page. To build this type of conditions you have to select "Advanced combinations" from the connections menu.

Once this step is also completed, you can decide to save the audience thus generated by checking the "Save this audience" box or proceed further and define the budget.

Budget definition

How much to spend on Facebook depends more on your pocket than on the tool itself. Usually the biggest risk entrepreneurs run is having a big budget and squandering it on poorly optimized campaigns. In fact, net of macroscopic errors, by investing so much money, the results tend to arrive even working in a rough way.

Clearly they would arrive more abundant if the campaign were professionally managed, but often one does not realize how many opportunities are being squandered, dazzled by the results that still continue to arrive.

My advice, therefore, is to start by investing a modest amount in relation to the total budget. Test different things using different target audiences and different types of advertisements. When you have identified the best performing combinations, push the accelerator and invest more money on them.

Daily budget and total budget

The first choice you need to make is to specify to Facebook how much money you want to invest in the campaign. You have two options:

- Daily budget. You are communicating to Facebook the amount you are willing to invest every day for your campaign. By using this type of budget you can avoid setting the date on which the campaign will end and therefore it will be up to you to deactivate it when you see fit.

● Total budget. In this case you set the total amount of expenditure that you are willing to incur. By selecting this mode you will be asked to set a start date and the date on which the campaign will end. It will be the Facebook algorithms to determine how to distribute the expenditure over the indicated period.

Which to use?

The criticism that is most often heard about the daily budget is that it tends to spend the expected money in any case, even at the cost of delivering the ad to that part of your target audience that rarely performs the action you are trying to achieve. To verify that this widespread belief was true, we tried to conduct a test by creating two identical campaigns in everything apart from the budget breakdown.

In one case we left the daily budget, in the other we set the total budget so that the subdivision of this along the duration would lead us to have a daily distribution identical to the daily budget set in the first case. Obviously, several factors may have intervened to change the performance of the two campaigns, but the total budget actually spent different figures depending on the days, leaving us to imagine a better optimization in the delivery of the advertisements.

On the other hand, the total budget generally requires a higher minimum investment threshold - at least five dollars per day - than can be set using the daily budget. In some cases we have created campaigns which, spending just 2 dollars per day, have still brought excellent results to the customer. To run them we necessarily had to use the daily budget, though.

Once these settings have been completed, we are ready to move on to the next step, which is the creation of the advertisements. Being a guide reserved for beginners, we do not dwell on the advanced options that you find immediately under the box we have just discussed. For now, just know that in the vast majority of cases the default settings are perfect.

Creating your Ads

We have finally arrived at the last, fundamental step in the construction of a new Facebook ads campaign: we are about to create an ad.

It is a very important step because, after having carefully defined who will be the target of our advertising activity, we now have to create the elements that will actually come into contact with the public. It is therefore natural that we will have to pay particular attention to all the characterizing aspects of the advertisements.

Now is the moment where the content strategy comes into play. If you don't have one yet, we suggest you read the previous chapters again before proceeding.

The first choice you can make is the ability to create a new ad or use an existing post and promote that. If the goal of the campaign is different from the promotion of a post, it is advisable to proceed with the creation of a new advertisement. The posts you publish on your fanpage are hardly optimized to perform at their best in an advertising campaign.

Standard or carousel listings

Proceeding with the creation of a new advertisement you will have to choose which format to use. You can select between only an image or a video in your advertisements (standard advertisements) or multiple images in an advertisement (carousel advertisements)

The substantial difference lies in the presentation of the visual, or the creative content present in the advertisement. In the first case, the image has a 16: 9 form factor and at the same time you have more space for the title and description of the content you are sharing. In the second one you can upload up to a maximum of five square images (1:1 ratio) which can then be browsed by pressing the side arrows. You will increase the visual impact while sacrificing space for the title and description.

Note that every single image of a carousel advertisement can direct the user to a specific address, so they are particularly effective advertisements if you want to promote e-commerce products. Also keep in mind that this format usually allows you to achieve generally better results in terms of CTR than traditional ads. This however does not mean that you will always have to use carousels anyway, as it all depends on your target audience. So our advice is - as always - to test and figure out which ads give the best results to your specific company or personal brand.

Creating an advertisement

Once you have selected the format of the new advertisement, you can proceed to its composition. In this case, let's see how to create a carousel since the process is slightly more complex and in any case allows us to also illustrate all the steps necessary to create a standard ad.

Link a page

First select a page to link to the ad you are creating. In this way, any interactions gained from the ad will increase the engagement of the selected page. Clearly you should select the page that represents the business you are promoting.

Create a copy

The next step is to create a copy. Depending on the type of campaign you have selected, you will have more or less characters available, in any case Facebook will inform you when you reach the maximum threshold.

Order of carousels and information card

If you have filled in the copy textbox, now you need to consider the two options related to images and links.

The first option (Automatically show first the links and images that get better results) allows Facebook algorithms to change the order of appearance of the images of the carousel ads in order to put in the first positions those with the best performance, that is, in the case of this specific campaign, those with the highest CTR.

The second option, on the other hand, allows you to decide whether to include an additional card reserved for your brand in your new carousel. It will therefore be a generic post that will show the profile image of the linked fanpage and a web address of your choice.

Visual and descriptions

Now it's time to create the visual part of the ad. As you can see, you have a selector at your disposal with which you can select each single slot that makes up the listing. For each of these you can select an image, a title, a description (this is the only optional field) and a destination URL.

In case you need more slots than the three open by default you will have to press the "+" button. As mentioned above, the maximum limit is five slots.

When creating the image for your ads, it is important to follow the former 20% rule, which states not to occupy more than 20% of the image with text.

The concept is very simple: Facebook prefers images to be images, not blocks of graphical text. So you can't cover the creatives you attach to your Facebook ADSs with promotional copy. At one time (until about a year ago) the 20% rule was in force, according to which the text could not cover more than twenty percent of the total surface of the image. It wasn't that easy to do the calculations by eye, and the verification tool sometimes did not work properly. It is suffice to say that once the limit was exceeded, the ad was rejected.

Recently Facebook replaced the old rule with a new mechanism.

For all images containing text for an area of less than 20% of the total, there are still no problems. For surpluses we no longer have the automatic rejection, but we have a progressive decrease in the potential reach with a consequent and inevitable increase in CPM. It is up to you to assess whether it can be convenient and whether any increase in performance is able to repay you for this initial gap.

There are many online tools that can evaluate the ratio between text and picture in your image. We recommend that you use them and still respect the old 20% rule for maximum results.

Call to action button

It seems like a trifle, but the call-to-action button is often able to significantly increase the CTR of your campaign. It is therefore a good practice to always select one whenever possible. The options that Facebook gives us for this ad element are the following.

- No buttons
- Buy now
- Book now
- Find out more
- Subscribe
- Download
- See more
- Request now
- Contact us

Whatever your choice, know that the button will direct the user to the address provided by the specific tab (in the case of carousel advertisements) or by the entire advertisement (in the case of a standard advertisement).

Preview and placement

As you have surely noticed during the entire creation phase, the Facebook ads interface creates a dynamic preview of the ad on the right side of the screen.

From this module, we can see the selected placements for our ads. These are the following.

● Computer News section. This ad format will be shown on the News Feed (the list of all posts) of target users who view Facebook using a personal computer

● News section of mobile devices. This format is reserved for target users who view their News Feed using smartphones or tablets

● Right column of computers. This format generates ads that will compose the right column that usually appears on every Facebook page. This format does not display the ads on mobile.

● Audience Network. This format allows you to occupy positions on mobile apps and websites that use the Facebook advertising network. In other words, your ads will appear outside the usual context of the social network

● Instagram. One of the latest Facebook ADS introductions. As you probably already know, Instagram is property of Facebook and for a few months now it has also been possible to take advantage of the most popular photo-centered social network in the world.

Check the previews and optimize the ads

First, always remember, to check the previews for any Facebook ads placements you decide to activate. Unfortunately, the length of the text portions is different for each format so you may end up with a perfect ad for the News Section on your computer but that performs poorly on mobile devices.

If your campaign has a high budget, you can consider the idea of creating specific ad groups for the various placements. If, on the other hand, you have to deal with a tight budget, it may not make sense to segment it further (remember that you must reserve a part of the budget for each group of ads) and therefore you will have to try to mediate between the characteristics of the various placements that you decide enable.

Which placements to enable?

Normally we recommend that you enable all of them and leave the performance statistics to judge the goodness of a placement. Much depends on the subject matter and the type of campaign you are creating. Facebook ADS is always ready to amaze you. On more than one occasion we have had unexpected results from the most unlikely placements (obviously unlikely according to our expectations).

It is therefore an excellent habit to never preclude yourself from any feature. The first few days of the campaign will serve you to fine-tune it and fix all the small imperfections that will inevitably crop up. Once the statistics highlight the less performing placements you can disable them and stick with what is performing.

We have finally finished the process of creating your new campaign. All you have to do is click on the "Order" button in order to submit it to the Facebook ADS team for approval. If you have done everything correctly this will arrive to them in a few minutes and in the following hours the advertisements will start to be displayed to the selected audience.

Chapter 17 - Facebook Pixel

At the beginning of the previous chapter, we have briefly talked about Facebook Pixel and how important it is to use it properly in order to maximize the impact of your campaigns. Let's dive a bit deeper and discover a bit more about it.

As always, let's start with a definition.

The Facebook pixel is a snippet of code that you can place on your website. It will collect the data with which you can measure conversions from your Facebook ads, optimize them, create your target audience for future campaigns and retarget users who have already performed an action on your website.

It works by activating cookies that have the task of monitoring user interactions on your website and in your Facebook ads.

In the past, there were two different types of Facebook pixels: the conversion pixel and the custom audience pixel. The former was abandoned by Facebook in 2017. Even if you used it in the past, now you have to switch to the new one. As this is a book for beginners, we assume you have no previous experience, so you are not affected by this change.

Why should you use the Facebook pixel?

The Facebook pixel gives you useful information to create more effective Facebook ads, targeting a personalized audience. With the data obtained from the Facebook pixel measurements, you always have the certainty that your ads are seen by people who, in all probability, will perform the action you want. This allows you to improve the conversion rate of your Facebook ads and get a higher ROI from social networks.

Not using Facebook Ads for your social media marketing strategy yet? Our advice is to install the Facebook pixel anyway right now. That way, you can start collecting the data you need right away when you're ready to create your first sponsored ad on Facebook.

Here are some ideas to make the most of the pixel and improve the results of your Facebook marketing campaigns.

Use Facebook Conversion Tracking

The Facebook pixel allows you to follow user interactions on your website after they have viewed your ad on Facebook.

You can even track customers across all of their devices. So you will be able to understand if they prefer to view your ads on mobile and perhaps switch to the desktop at the time of purchase. This information can help you refine your advertising strategy and calculate your return on investment in a much more accurate way.

Use Facebook retargeting

Facebook pixel retargeting data and dynamic ads allow you to show personalized ads to people who have already visited your site. And here you can be really precise. For example, you can show the ad of the specific product that the person in question had abandoned in the cart or added to the wish list on your website.

Create similar audiences

Facebook is able to use its targeting data to help you build an audience of people with similar tastes, interests and ages to those of the audience already interacting with your website. This way, you can broaden your potential customer base.

Optimize Facebook Ads for Conversions

Without a pixel, the only conversions you can optimize for are link clicks. The pixel, on the other hand, allows you to optimize your ads for conversions more akin to your business goals, such as purchases and subscriptions.

Optimize Facebook ads for value

By collecting data on who buys your products or services and how much they spend on your website, Facebook can optimize the audience of your ads based on its value. In other words, your ads will automatically be shown to those most likely to make higher-value purchases.

Get more tools and metrics

Do you want to use conversion campaigns on the web, custom audiences from your site or dynamic ads? All this is only possible if you install the Facebook pixel. The pixel can also be useful in measuring metrics such as cost per lead or cost per conversion.

How to use the Facebook pixel

You can use the Facebook pixel to collect data relating to two types of events. Facebook has predefined a series of 17 standard events, but you can always set up your own custom events.

An "event" is nothing more than a specific action performed by a visitor on your website. For example, making a purchase.

Facebook Pixel Standard Events

The 17 Facebook pixel standard events for which just copy and paste the standard event code are the following.

1. Buy: When someone completes a purchase on your website.

1. Lead: When someone signs up for a trial or otherwise identifies themselves as a contact on your website.

1. Complete registration: when someone completes a registration form on your website, such as a registration.

1. Add payment info: when someone enters their payment details during the purchase process on your website.

1. Add to Cart: When someone adds a product to their cart on your website.

1. Add to wishlist: When someone adds a product to the wishlist on your website.

1. Start Checkout: When someone initiates the process of going to checkout during a purchase on your website.

1. Search: When someone uses the Search feature to find an article on your site.

1. View Content: When someone lands on a specific page on your website.

1. Contact us: when someone contacts your business.

1. Personalize the product: when someone selects a specific version of the product, for example a certain color.

1. Donate: When someone makes a donation to your cause.

1. Find position: when someone searches for the physical location of your company.

1. Schedule: When someone books an appointment at your company.

1. Start Trial: When someone signs up to try your product for free.

1. Submit Request: When someone requests your specific product, service or program, such as a credit card.

1. Subscribe: When someone subscribes to a paid product or service.

Additional details can be added to standard events using code snippets called parameters. These allow you to customize standard events based on:

- Value of the conversion event
- Currency
- Content type or ID
- Cart contents

For example, you can use Facebook's measurement pixel to record views of a specific category on your website, rather than measuring all views across the board. Let's say you own a pet supplies website; you may want to separate dog owners from cat owners based on the sections of the site viewed and the Facebook Pixel allows you to do just that.

Facebook Pixel Custom Events

You can use custom events instead of standard ones to gather more detail than the basic ones can offer.

Custom events use URL rules based on specific URLs or URL keywords. Again, this is an extremely advanced feature that you will rarely use in your social media marketing campaign. Therefore, we have decided to leave it as it is important that you focus on the most important information first.

How to create a Facebook pixel to add to your website

Now that you know what to monitor and why, it's time to create your pixel and make it work on your website.

Step 1: create your pixel

- From your Facebook Events Manager, click on the hamburger icon (≡) at the top left and select Pixel

- Click on the green Create a Pixel button

- Give your pixel a name, type the URL of your website and click Create

When choosing the name for your pixel, remember that, with Events Manager, you only have one pixel for each ad account. The name should represent your business and not a specific campaign. If you want to use more than one pixel per ad account, you can do so with Facebook Business Manager.

Step 2: add the pixel code to your website

At this point, in order to make your pixel work and have it collect information on your website, you need to install some codes on your web pages. There are various ways to do this, depending on the web platform used.

If you use an ecommerce platform like Squarespace or a tag manager like Google Tag Manager, you can directly install your pixel without having to change your website code.

If you work with a developer or other experts who can help you edit your web code, click Email Developer Instructions to send all the information needed to install the pixel.

If none of the above cases are yours, you will need to insert the pixel code directly into your web pages. Below we will guide you step by step.

- Click on Install the code manually

- Copy and paste the pixel code into your website title code. In other words, post it after the <head> tag, but before the </head> tag. You will need to paste it on every page or in your template (if you have one).

• Decide whether to use automatic advanced matching. This option allows you to associate Facebook profiles with customer data collected on your website. This allows you to track conversions much more accurately and create larger audiences of customers.

• Check if you have correctly installed the code by entering the URL of your website and clicking on Send test traffic.

Your Facebook pixel is ready to track activities. Now click on "Continue" to go to step 3.

Step 3: Monitor the right events for your business

Choose which of the 17 standard events you want to monitor using the toggle buttons. For each event, you will have to choose between monitoring when the page is loaded or monitoring the action online. Here is the difference between the two options.

• Page loading monitoring. The feature monitors actions such as visiting a new page, placing a like on the completion of a purchase or terminating the subscription on a page.

• Online action monitoring. This feature monitors the actions performed within the page (such as clicking on the "add to cart" button), which do not open a new page.

Also, you can set parameters for certain events. For example, in case you want to track purchases of a specific dollar value.

If you want to use Facebook Pixel Custom Events, go to your Facebook Events Manager.

Select Custom Conversions from the top left menu. Then click Create Custom Conversion to define your custom conversion event using URL rules.

Step 4: Confirm that your Facebook pixel is working properly

Previously, you tested the installation of your Facebook pixel by sending test traffic. In any case, before collecting and analyzing the data from your Facebook pixel, send confirmation of its correct functioning.

Add the Facebook Pixel Helper extension to your Google Chrome browser. (Available exclusively for Chrome; if you are using a different browser, you must install Chrome to use the Pixel Helper)

Visit the page where you installed the Facebook pixel. If the extension finds the pixel, the </> icon will turn blue and a popup will tell you how many pixels it found on the page. The popup will also tell you if your pixel is working correctly. Otherwise, it will provide you with the error data, in order to allow you to correct it.

Step 5: Add the pixel notification to your website

As required by Facebook's terms of use (and applicable regulations), you must let your website visitors know that you are collecting their data.

In other words, you must clearly communicate that you are using the Facebook pixel and that the data could be collected through cookies or other methods. You must also let users know that they can refuse consent to the collection of data concerning them.

Please, do not overlook this last step even if your personal brand or company is relatively small. Privacy is extremely important and following these rules will give you peace of mind.

Conclusion

Congratulations on making it to the very end of this book, it has been a great journey.

We hope you were able to find valuable information to improve the online presence of your company or personal brand using the power of Facebook marketing. We have tried our best to give you every tool and strategy you might need to turn your business page into a money making machine.

Now it is on you to put in practice what you have learned. Because remember that understanding a concept and making it work for you are two totally different things and as an entrepreneur or influencer you should always be willing to take the risk to try and test new strategies.

We are sure that if you commit to seriously working on your Facebook marketing strategy, you will be well ahead of competition. After all, it is not a secret that most businesses have a superficial approach when it comes to their online presence, especially on Facebook. Doing things differently will certainly put you miles ahead of them and will give you an unfair advantage in the long run.

We hope you enjoyed this book and we wish you great success!

www.ingramcontent.com/pod-product-compliance
Lightning Source LLC
Chambersburg PA
CBHW061016050326
40689CB00012B/2662